art quilt
maps

CAPTURE A SENSE OF PLACE WITH FIBER COLLAGE—A VISUAL GUIDE

Valerie S. Goodwin

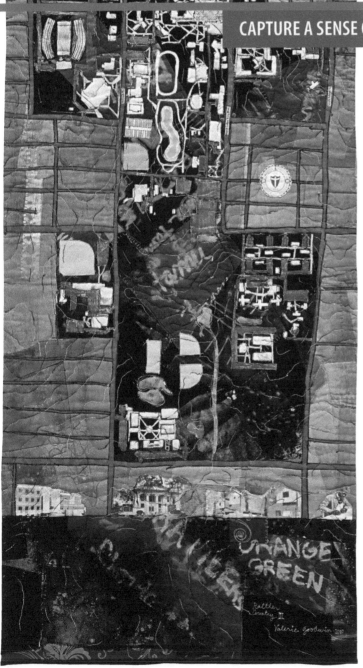

C&T PUBLISHING

Text and Photography copyright © 2013 by Valerie S. Goodwin

Photography copyright © 2013 by C&T Publishing, Inc.

Publisher: Amy Marson

Creative Director: Gailen Runge

Art Director: Kristy Zacharias

Editor: Lynn Koolish

Technical Editors: Priscilla Read and Gailen Runge

Cover Designers: Christina Jarumay Fox and April Mostek

Book Designer: Christina Jarumay Fox

Production Coordinators: Jenny Davis and Rue Flaherty

Production Editor: Joanna Burgarino

Photo Assistant: Mary Peyton Peppo

Quilt and Art Photography by Christina Carty-Francis and Diane Pedersen of C&T Publishing, Inc., unless otherwise noted; How-To Photography by Robert T. Goodwin Jr., unless otherwise noted

Published by C&T Publishing, Inc., P.O. Box 1456, Lafayette, CA 94549

Library of Congress Cataloging-in-Publication Data

Goodwin, Valerie S., 1954-

 Art quilt maps : capture a sense of place with fiber collage : a visual guide / Valerie S. Goodwin.

   pages cm

 ISBN 978-1-60705-682-9 (soft cover)

1. Patchwork--Patterns. 2. Quilting--Patterns. 3. Fabric pictures. I. Title.

TT835.G6699 2013

746.46--dc23

                          2013000947

10 9 8 7 6 5 4 3 2 1

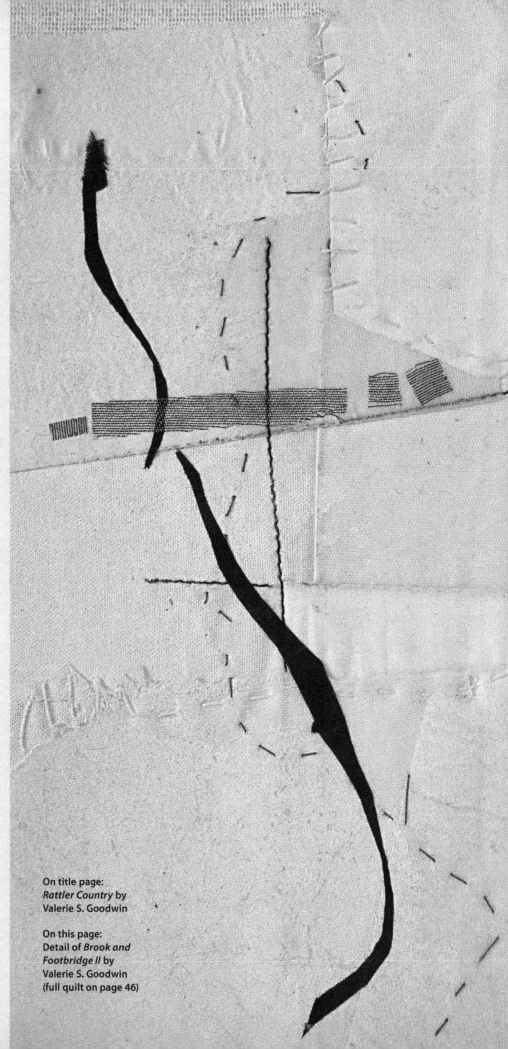

On title page:
Rattler Country by Valerie S. Goodwin

On this page:
Detail of *Brook and Footbridge II* by Valerie S. Goodwin
(full quilt on page 46)

ACKNOWLEDGMENTS

Many thanks go out to C&T Publishing for giving me the platform to write this book. Susanne Woods deserves special appreciation for her efforts to introduce me to the C&T team. I would also like to thank Diane Pedersen, Lynn Koolish, and all the other staff for giving me expert guidance through the publication process.

Deep affection must be expressed here to my mother, Ella, and father, James, for all of the sacrifices they made and love they gave me over the years.

I want to offer heartfelt appreciation and love to the rest of my family for their role in giving me the space and time to write this book. Many family members generously stepped up and made sacrifices so that I could dedicate myself to this exciting and challenging undertaking.

In addition, I am grateful to my students for their contributions to this book. I am so fortunate that the quilters who took my classes across the country and my talented architecture students at the Florida A&M University School of Architecture took a leap of faith and tackled the work you see in this book.

And last but definitely not least, heartfelt thanks and love to Bob, my dear husband. He was so encouraging and helped to photograph the work you see in this book.

contents

introduction:
mapping my beginnings as a quilt artist

I became interested in quilting quite by accident. I read an article in an academic journal that described a design project in which architecture students were asked to design a museum for quilts. Maybe the voice of my maternal grandmother, a home economics teacher, whispered to me as I read every word in the article. Perhaps it sparked a memory of learning to sew during hot and humid summers while on vacation at my grandmother's home in Tuscumbia, Alabama, during the 1960s. Whatever it was, I feel fortunate to have found the kernel of possibilities the day I read the article.

From that day onward, I began a journey that has taken me in many surprising and unexpected directions. It also created an interesting tension—could aspects of quilting transfer to the way I teach architecture? The core question for me was, should a real architect quilt? Would I still be taken seriously as an architect? I received my architectural education in a male-dominated field in a male-dominated world. My exposure to the women's liberation movement during the late 1960s and 1970s created a feeling that quilting was somehow counter to the advancement of women in our society. There were all sorts of reservations spinning around in my brain. Deep down, though, I think I knew I might be onto something.

Despite these reservations, I plowed ahead with the determination I inherited from Mother Scruggs, my paternal grandmother. I thought about many things she instilled in me. She was a force of nature.

Mama Steele, my maternal grandmother
Photo by Valerie S. Goodwin

The next semester I created a number of design exercises for my beginning architecture students. They studied the design principles and elements seen in traditional patchwork blocks such as Nine-Patch, Flying Geese, and Log Cabin. As part of the project, they designed quilt blocks made from colored paper. The students then created small works of architecture that would display their quilt blocks.

Project by Donald Gray, architecture student, 1999

The students seemed to respond well to this unique way of learning about architecture and design. At times I now incorporate quilting into other architecture classes. Quilting is indeed like building; one constructs a quilt like one constructs an architectural design. Wherever I can, I weave ideas about art and craft into courses I teach across the curriculum.

LEARNING TO SEW AND QUILT

Many years earlier, I had abandoned my interest in sewing, partly in an effort to conform to peer pressure in high school. As I grew older, the desire to cope in a male-dominated profession left me with the feeling that working with bricks and mortar was a more noble goal than working with fabric and thread.

But fortunately, memories of the fun and satisfaction I felt when my grandmother taught me to sew spurred me forward.

Mother Scruggs, my paternal grandmother
Photo courtesy of Valerie S. Goodwin

I also thought about Cousin Hattie, who lived with my mother's family during the 1940s and 1950s. This remarkable woman made hundreds of quilts that she pieced during the summer and quilted during the winter. Many family members who are lucky enough to have her amazing quilts cherish her legacy. It was hard to ignore this deep-rooted heritage of working with fabric. These feelings and experiences prompted me to take a quilting workshop.

In 1998 I learned to quilt by enrolling in a six-week class in quiltmaking at a local community college. I made a sampler quilt totally by hand. It is hard to describe what this experience did for me—all I can say is that it set off a series of light bulbs in my creative psyche. Shortly after this, a friend shared with me a copy of the 1999 Quilt National exhibit catalog. A whole world of possibilities was revealed! From then on, my goal was to discover how I could combine my love of architectural design with the medium of quiltmaking. The answer to my initial question is overwhelmingly apparent: Yes, real architects can and *do* quilt!

mapping out
ways of working

SOURCES OF INSPIRATION

As with many artists, I am influenced by so many things—the visual world has an abundance of inspiration. I have a passion for art, architecture, and maps—the language of lines, shapes, and color captures my imagination. My map compositions reflect these varied interests.

I love to design maps of real and imaginary landscapes and cities. Aerial views, with their lines and shapes, intrigue me. Repeatedly I refer to books on quilts, art, maps, urban planning, and site design. Travel is definitely something I do when I can. I have a bucket list of famous places I want to visit one day, and it prompted me to make the following quilts, one of a real place (*The Acropolis*) and one of a place that exists only in my imagination (*Unknown Regions I*).

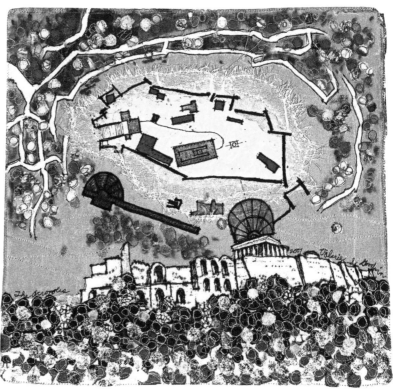

The Acropolis by Valerie S. Goodwin, 2007, 13″ × 12.75″,
in the private collection of Deborah Cashett
Photo by Richard Brunck

Unknown Regions I by Valerie S. Goodwin, 2003, 10″ × 15″

Photo by Richard Brunck

I am always bookmarking interesting sites and maps on the Internet so I can find them again. When I find a map of a place that I am interested in, I spend time looking at it to think about what I like about it. Sometimes the lines interest me. At other times, the shapes or the colors, and even the topography, capture my attention.

I also have a nice little collection of books with plenty of ideas for possible fiber-art maps. In my opinion, most inspiration comes from curiosity. As a woman who is an artist, I have learned the importance of being a hunter-gatherer of things I find creative. The following is my list of things that inspire my fiber-art maps. While my list may seem to include unrelated interests, for me they all work together. What topics would you add or take away to fit your background and interests?

- maps
- nature
- poetry
- photos of aerial views
- art
- architectural drawings, urban design
- typography and calligraphy

WHY MAPS?

A map is an abstract idea of a place; it is a drawing, an interpretation of reality based on what the map maker wants to show. Map makers make choices about what to include as well as what to leave out—accordingly, a map is a reflection of its maker and how it will be used. There are many, many types of maps. Architects and other design professionals are one type of map makers. We use maps to communicate information to contractors, clients, the public, and other audiences through the various drawings we create, such as site maps, design sketches, and construction documents. Other types of maps include these:

- Road maps that show major highways
- Road maps that show streets and alleys
- Tourist maps that show landmarks of interest
- Utility company maps that depict a neighborhood's gas and electric lines

The scale of a map is important: If the scale is small, the map can include more detail, for example, streets and alleys; if the scale is large, it might be able to show just the major highways.

Another way that maps interpret reality is through the use of symbols. Maps use marks and figures, such as points, lines, area patterns, and colors. These elements can be the tools for making a fiber-art map come to life.

Examples of lines and shapes
Drawing by Dario McPhee

USING ARCHITECTURE AS DESIGN INSPIRATION

My experience in architecture guides much of what I do as an artist, and I tap into my architectural background in many ways. For example, I take pleasure in seeing how cities are organized. Like many things around us, cities have characteristics that describe their style. There are places that were designed using an orderly grid, such as Savannah, Georgia. Other places, such as Madrid, Spain, are laid out in a more casual way.

Orderly grids of Savannah, Georgia
Drawing courtesy of Eric J. Jenkins, author of To Scale: One Hundred Urban Plans

Casual plan of Madrid, Spain
Drawing courtesy of Eric J. Jenkins, author of To Scale: One Hundred Urban Plans

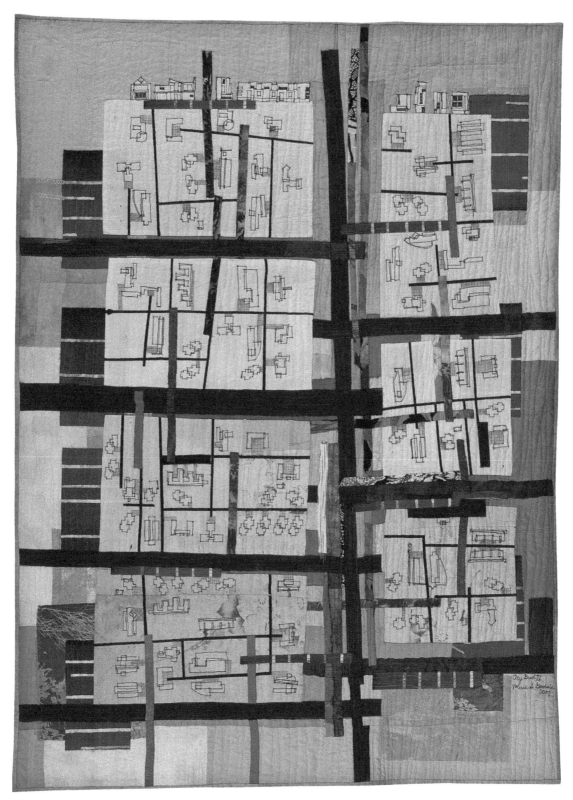

City Grid IV by Valerie S. Goodwin, 2007, 39″ × 46″

Photo by Richard Brunck

This quilt uses a rigid system of lines and shapes based
on those found in a place such as Savannah.

City Grid II **by Valerie S. Goodwin**
2001, 39″ × 46″
Photo by Richard Brunck

This quilt has a much more organic structure, such as you would see in a city like Madrid.

ARCHITECT VERSUS ARTIST

There are times when I work as many architects do—after the design phase, work proceeds in a linear sequence without many detours until the building is complete. There are few opportunities to veer off the path, since there are many players in this process and many real-life responsibilities.

By comparison, artists have more leeway and thus the opportunity to work more loosely. If they choose, artists can let the design process evolve. Improvisation, rather than planning out every detail, becomes the guiding force. This way of designing is relatively new for me, but I find it to be very fruitful. It helps me to be more open to free association and thus allows many different ideas to seep in. As a result, my work is now more abstract. I also appreciate that as an artist, I am working with my hands directly on the materials that create the work.

THE BEST OF BOTH WORLDS

Both ways of creating are valid given the differing circumstances. But a combined approach seems to work well for me. *City Grid II* started with a small drawing, but the design evolved and shifted during the process of making the quilt. I think I gave myself this freedom because it was a map of an imaginary place.

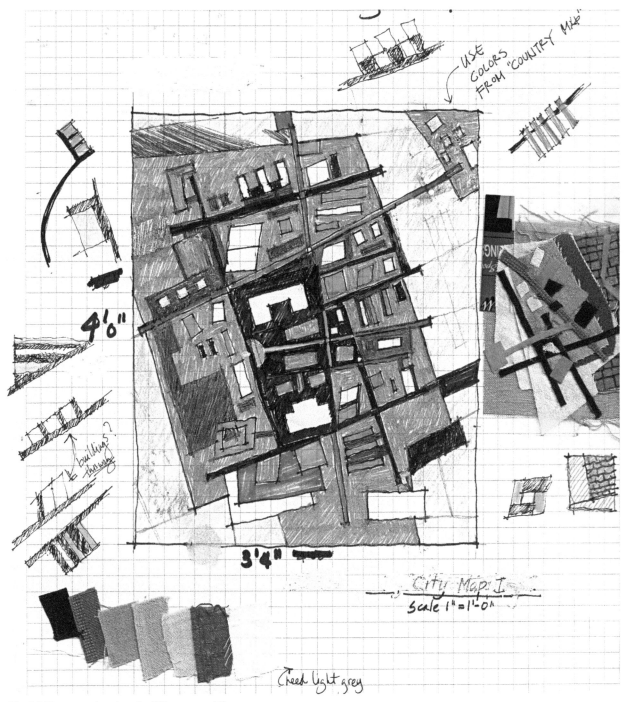

City Grid II **process drawings (quilt is on page 14)**

In contrast, *Lay of the Land I*, a map of a real place, began with many sketches, very small at first. I played with the composition of the various maps that I wanted to use. It was important to tell the story of this place in a poetic way but with a degree of accuracy. After sketching, I auditioned fabrics, started working with the materials, and then let my intuition guide me!

Another way I design is to combine inspiration from art and architecture. Artists such as Franz Kline, Jackson Pollock, and Robert Motherwell interest me, especially their black, white, and gray paintings. Their energetic use of line and shape communicates feeling.

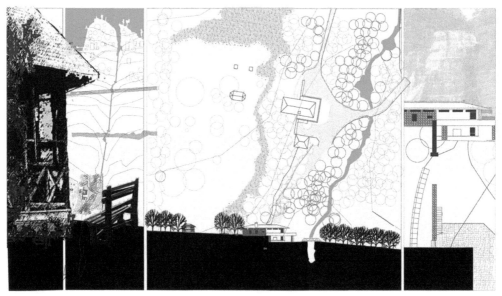

Lay of the Land I **process drawings**

Lay of the Land I **by Valerie S. Goodwin, 2010, 31½″ × 20½″**

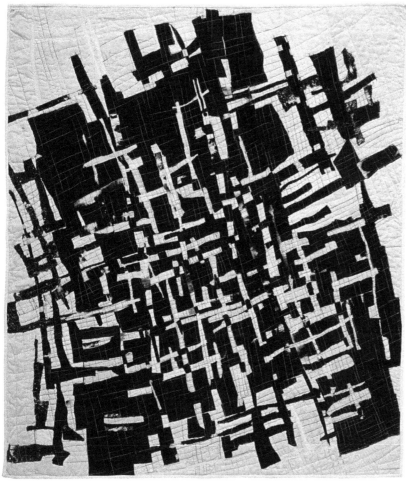

Organic Grid II by Valerie S. Goodwin, 2001, 36" × 42"

For a time I experimented with limiting myself to black, white, and gray fabric.

These black-and-white quilts were influenced by maps, actually one map in particular. In the eighteenth century, Pope Benedict XIV asked Giambattista Nolli, an Italian architect and surveyor, to engrave a map of Rome that has become famous. Nolli created this masterpiece in 1748.

The Nolli Map was a big eye-opener for me! It is so simple, pure, and striking. It is one of my favorite kinds of architectural maps because it simplifies a map down to two things: *black* and *white*. It shows enclosed/private spaces (black) versus open/public spaces (white).

It is hard to resist the simplicity and sophistication of black and white. My architectural students created an amazing patchwork (pages 84 and 85) based on the Nolli Map (page 18). One day I want to create my own personal Nolli Map of a familiar place.

Limiting the color palette to black, white, and gray made the lines and shapes do most of the work to create a very expressive design.

Ground Zero by Valerie S. Goodwin, 2001, 49" × 35"

Nolli Map created by Giambattista Nolli
Drawing of the Nolli Map courtesy of Fredrick H. Zal, www.FHZal.com

CLOSING THOUGHTS

I hope this chapter has given you ideas about gathering inspiration from many sources, no matter how unusual and unrelated they may seem. I encourage you to revel in the freedom of making unexpected connections. Keep looking for inspiration; it's everywhere!

LOOKING AHEAD

The following chapters explain the tools and materials needed and then guide you through a series of exercises or practices that offer opportunities to make design decisions about how to artistically represent elements in fiber-art map quilts. Technique and design exercises are included, intended to help you create fiber-art maps from different perspectives. You can explore creating maps from your imagination and those that interpret a real place. By the end of this book you'll have plenty of food for thought and a path toward creating your own personal map quilts.

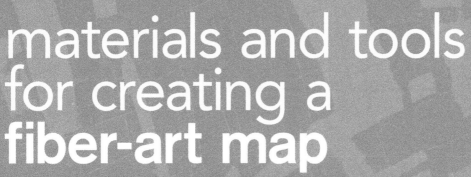

materials and tools
for creating a
fiber-art map

The quilts in this book are made up of layers of collaged fabric, paint, and thread. This combination of materials and techniques allows you to work fluidly. Fusing is another important method because it gives you the ability to cut small elements and secure them to the surface of the map.

BASIC EQUIPMENT FOR SEWING, CUTTING, AND FUSING

Iron and ironing board

Sewing machine: In good working order with a free-motion foot

Nonstick (Teflon) sheet or Silicone Release Paper: For use with fusible web

Medium-sized rotary cutter: For cutting fabric

Gridded rotary cutting ruler: For use with the rotary cutter

Plastic gridded ruler: For measuring and drawing straight lines

Thimble: For hand stitching

Needles: For hand sewing

Pins

Pencil sharpener

Medium to large scissors: For cutting medium to large pieces of fabric

Small fabric scissors: For cutting small pieces of fabric

Small scissors: For cutting paper and cardboard

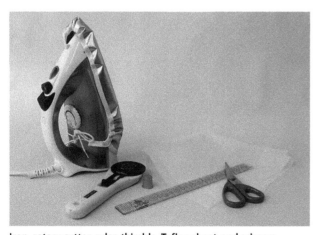

Iron, rotary cutter, ruler, thimble, Teflon sheet, and scissors

 TIP

I use and recommend the Ironslide Iron Shoe by Bo-Nash. It has a nonstick fiberglass surface that protects both the iron and the fabric, decreasing the incidence of burns or scorches and preventing fusibles from sticking to the iron.

Fusible web: For securing small pieces. There are many brands, but I prefer Mistyfuse because it is lightweight and very sheer; it doesn't add bulk to a fused piece, and it bonds well after it cools. I use both black and white Mistyfuse.

Decorative threads: For hand sewing; use ones that you like.

Threads: For machine sewing and quilting; select colors that work for the project.

Monofilament or invisible thread: For stitches that can't be seen

Thin batting: I use low-loft polyester batting.

Number 2 lead pencil and rolling ball pens: For sketching ideas

Permanent, waterproof archival pens: For writing text and drawing lines. You should have a range from very thin to very thick (005, 01, 02, 03, 04, 05, and 08). I prefer Fabrico permanent pens for adding splashes of color. They come in a variety of colors.

Blank index cards (3″ × 5″) and sketchbooks: For sketching ideas

TRANSFER AND STENCIL SUPPLIES

Poster board or cardstock: For making stencils

Wax-free tracing paper: For transferring map shapes and lines. I prefer the Saral Transfer Paper variety pack. It includes colors that will stand out against most fabric colors. It can be purchased online from many sources.

Craft knife, such as an X-Acto, and blades:
For cutting stencils

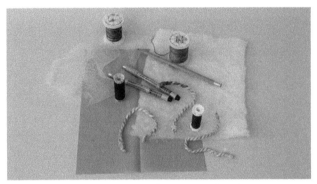

Wax-free tracing paper; batting; fusible web; thread; permanent, waterproof archival pens; number 2 lead pencil; and hand-dyed threads

FABRICS AND STABILIZERS

I love patterned fabrics, but I tend not to use them very much. I like to think of fabrics as tubes of paint; I build up patterns with individual solid fabrics. When I do use printed fabric, I use it subtly for texture or pattern.

Crinoline: For stabilizing. Make sure to buy the stiff, 100% cotton type, not the type you might see in a prom dress.

Crinoline

Various commercial solid fabrics and hand-dyed fabrics: 100% cotton. Have a good variety of values: light, medium, and dark.

Commercial solid fabrics and hand-dyed fabrics

Silk organza: For layering and transparency. Use white, off-white, or other colors as desired. Do not use synthetic organza—it tends to scorch easily.

Various sheer drapery scraps: Look for interesting subtle patterns or florals for layering and transparency.

Kimono scraps: Hand-dyed or painted fabric that has been recycled from a Japanese kimono. I recommend solids or small, understated patterns. (*Optional*)

Silk organza, sheer drapery scraps, and kimono scraps

PAINTING SUPPLIES

Paint can be used in many ways on fiber-art map quilts.

Inexpensive brushes: Use brushes that suit your work, such as foam brushes, flat art brushes, house painter's brushes, inexpensive sponge brushes, or foam stencil brushes.

Fabric paints or acrylic paints combined with a fabric medium: I prefer Liquitex Soft Body Artist Acrylics, which have a very creamy, easy-to-apply texture. The fabric medium helps to soften the acrylic paint for use on fabric.

Acrylic ink

Plastic cups or plates: For mixing paint

Inexpensive rubber gloves: To protect hands

Garbage bag or other plastic: To protect the work surface

Painter's tape: To mask paint on fabric

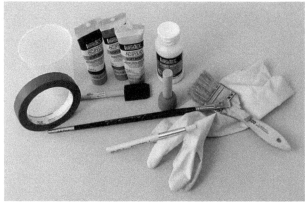

Plastic cup, blue painter's tape, soft-body acrylic paint, brushes, and rubber gloves

STAMPING SUPPLIES

There are many objects to use for stamping shapes such as buildings, trees, and so on. After you've done this a few times, I bet you'll add your own ideas to this list.

Straws: The ends are great for making small circular marks, like those you might use to represent trees.

Basswood or balsa wood sticks: Come in various sizes and profiles: round, square, and rectangular; use them to make shapes and lines.

Craft foam: Use to make your own stamps.

Pushpins: Use to make small circular shapes.

Small objects: Anything that you might be able to make a line or shape with when you have dipped it in paint

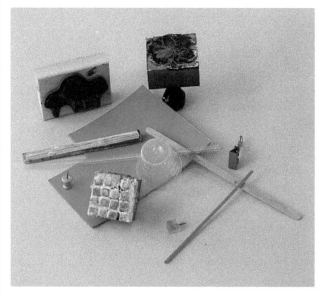

Commercial stamps, wood sticks, straws, pushpins, craft foam, plastic cup, and binder clip

background music:
the landscape layer

Now that you have an understanding of the supplies and materials used to create fiber-art maps, let's get into the process. This chapter will show you how to create the background or landscape layer—the surface where the streets, houses, forests, rivers, and so on will be placed. A beautiful surface sets the tone for each map.

After finishing this surface, I am sometimes tempted to think of it as a finished piece. That is because this technique can create a wonderful play of texture and color. But for map making, it is just the beginning step. Later in this chapter, you will see some examples of approaches for creating different types of landscapes.

> **NOTE**
>
> *As you work through the exercises and examples in this book, remember that you are building a framework to create your own unique map art.*

MATERIALS

Basic equipment and supplies for sewing, cutting, and fusing (page 20)

Fabrics and stabilizers: Crinolines, solids, silk organzas, and sheers (page 21)

Painting supplies (page 22)

THE OPAQUE LAYER

1. To begin a practice piece, cut a piece of crinoline just a bit bigger than the intended size of the finished map. I use this material because of its stiff yet lightweight quality. It also helps to keep the quilt stable and flat.

2. Add casually-cut shapes of fabric to the crinoline using a sew-and-flip technique. To do this, place the first piece of fabric right side up on the crinoline. Add the next piece facing the first one, right side down. Machine stitch in place (along one edge) with contrasting thread. Flip open and press. Continue adding pieces until the desired area is covered. As you add a piece, try extending the stitches beyond it. This makes interesting marks in the "land."

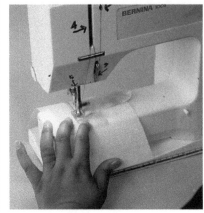

The sew-and-flip process

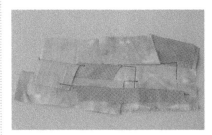

Completed sew-and-flip step

For the best effect, select fabrics that will not compete with the key elements of the map design, such as the roads, buildings, and so on. Play with the arrangement and be sure to shift the fabric placement as needed to overlap each piece. Don't try to control it too much—just play! Create a pleasing arrangement and pin the fabrics in place so you will know where they go, or work spontaneously, adding and arranging the fabric as you sew each piece.

3. Leave any free edges raw. Use a hand-sewn running stitch or an interesting hand embroidery stitch to secure these edges to the rest of the fabric.

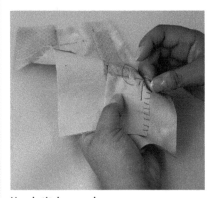

Hand stitch raw edges.

 TIPS

Do *not* feel that you have to make this layer realistic. In other words, we know that healthy grass is generally green, but shades of purple on the landscape could be effective as an abstract interpretation of the earth's surface.

Shift and overlap the fabric pieces to add more interest and variety.

Sew down the raw edges using embroidery stitches that are not tightly packed together—try a herringbone or blanket stitch.

THE PAINTED LAYER

1. Protect your work surface from the paint.

2. You can use fabric paint or acrylic paint. If you use the latter, combine it with an acrylic fabric medium to keep the fabric from becoming too stiff. Follow the manufacturer's instructions carefully. Water down the paint with a ratio of one part water to three parts paint as a starting point. Apply the watered-down paint to portions of the fabric surface. Do not cover all the fabric with paint. You want to allow most of the fabric to peek through.

Experiment with colors that provide interesting effects. One approach is to pick a color in the same value range and hue as the fabrics you have used so far. After you've completed painting, allow the paint to dry, and then iron the fabric to heat set the paint.

Paint fabric.

PAINTING TIPS

You might want to pick a color that is a shade darker or lighter than the fabrics.

Another choice is white paint that has been enhanced with a bit of color found in the main fabric.

Add various shapes by masking off areas using painter's tape (page 35).

Experiment with a foam brush, flat art brush, house painter's brush, or inexpensive sponge for different effects.

Apply the paint across two adjacent fabrics that are different colors. This step helps to blend the colors and minimize abrupt changes in color.

THE TRANSLUCENT LAYER

The goal of this step is to add the richness of layering and transparency to the background.

1. Select a sheer fabric for layering. Try picking something close in value or hue to the background fabric. Silk organza works better than synthetic because it does not have a shiny finish and it is less prone to burning or melting when ironed.

2. Prepare small pieces of the sheer fabric by backing them with your preferred brand of fusible web. (For more on using fusibles, see Fusing, page 31.)

3. Pin the sheer layering fabric in place. When you are satisfied with the placement, iron it to the surface. Fusing enhances the watercolor or layering effect because it keeps the sheer fabric flat against the fabric underneath.

4. Sew around the exposed edges by machine with a free-motion foot. This step doesn't take much time, but it is an effective way of adding understated complexity and drama to the surface you are creating. Stitching around each edge of the fused fabric also helps ensure that it stays in place over time.

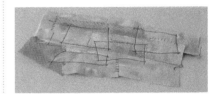

Silk organza with dark edge stitching

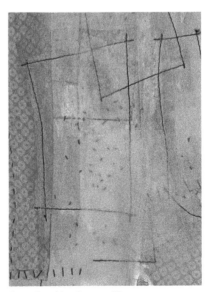

Completed background layer

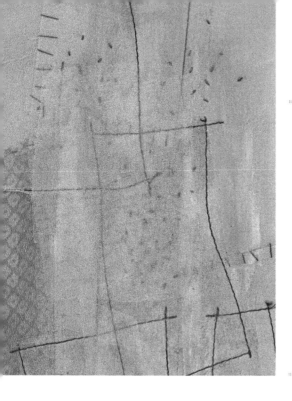

PICKING THE RIGHT SHEER

If your background colors are in the medium-to-dark value range, white or off-white silk organza can make a beautiful watercolor effect. White or off-white silk organza will not stand out as much on fabric that is in the light value range.

Applying sheer fabric across bordering fabrics helps to blend the colors and to reduce abrupt changes in color.

Collect sheer drapery scraps with interesting subtle patterns and use them with or instead of the silk organza.

Alter the color of organza by painting it with watered-down fabric paint before you add it to the background.

MAKING THE STITCHING STAND OUT

Add hand stitching to areas away from the raw edges of each piece. This technique helps to add texture across the landscape. Try seed stitches and French knots.

If you want the stitches to stand out, use contrasting, thick thread. If you want the stitches to blend in or be subtle, use thin threads and colors that are close in hue to the background fabric.

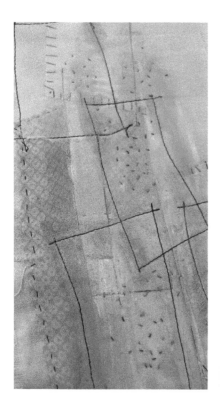

Add hand stitching for texture across landscape.

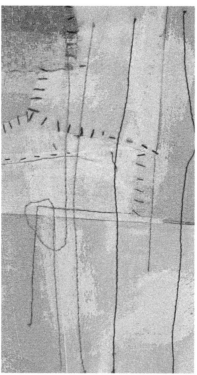

Dark, medium, and light thread against light background

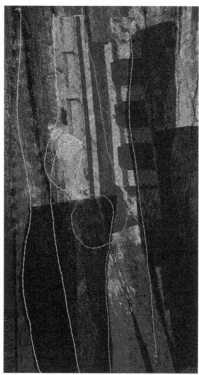

Dark, medium, and light thread against dark background

MORE BACKGROUNDS

Different types of maps require different types of backgrounds, each having its own characteristics. Below are three examples that I have done. How would you approach creating each of them?

A landscape with lines and movement

A landscape with an organic feeling, lots of repetition, and curves

A landscape made up of squares and rectangles with elements that are parallel and perpendicular as well as shapes with hard edges

Linear landscape

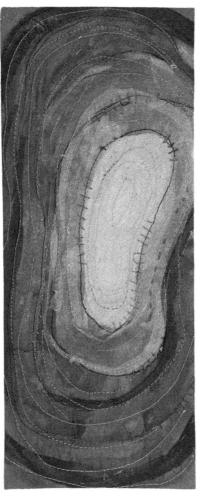

Organic landscape

Rectilinear landscape

As you create your own maps, you'll begin by creating a background that supports your vision. There is no set way to create a background—improvise, be flexible, and let the technique evolve as you become more confident with the process. Be open to trying many variations based on your specific design intent. Above all, think, design, and play!

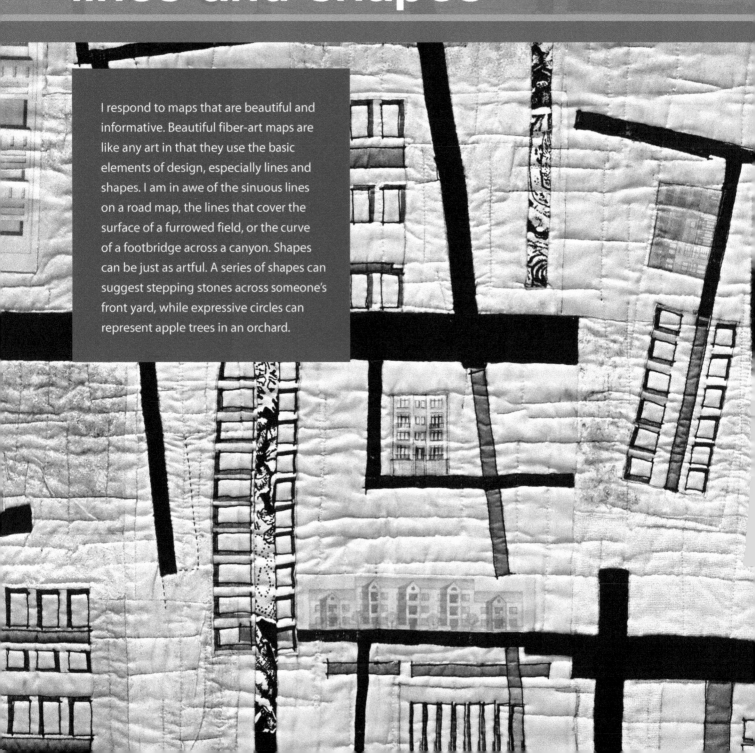

putting it on the map:
techniques to create
lines and shapes

I respond to maps that are beautiful and informative. Beautiful fiber-art maps are like any art in that they use the basic elements of design, especially lines and shapes. I am in awe of the sinuous lines on a road map, the lines that cover the surface of a furrowed field, or the curve of a footbridge across a canyon. Shapes can be just as artful. A series of shapes can suggest stepping stones across someone's front yard, while expressive circles can represent apple trees in an orchard.

In this chapter we'll focus on ways to create lines and shapes—the design elements at the heart of the map that communicate the information that brings the map to life. These lines and shapes are added on top of the background or landscape layer that you learned to create in the previous chapter.

When creating a fiber-art map based on a real or imaginary place, a good exercise is to imagine how lines and shapes on the map will symbolize the natural and human-made ingredients that are the heart of the map. These lines and shapes can be so appealing and create such beauty; together they send messages about what you want the work to say about a place.

There are many ways to make the lines and shapes of a map. You may already be familiar with some of the techniques, such as hand and machine sewing. Various mixed-media techniques such as painting, fusing, and collage are good alternatives. Based on this chapter, you might want to make a series of samples with the various techniques. It will serve as a valuable reference tool for map making.

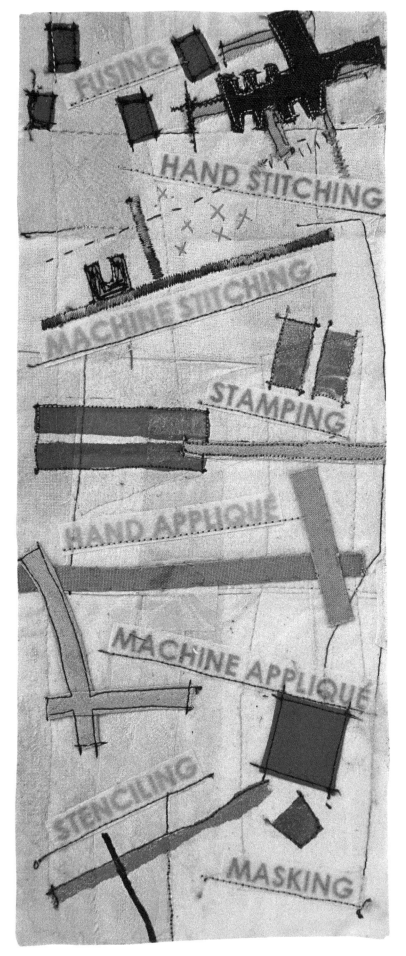

Putting It on the Map
by Valerie S. Goodwin,
2012, 3″ × 11″

Lines and shapes

MATERIALS

Basic equipment and supplies for sewing, cutting, and fusing (page 20)

Fabrics and stabilizers: crinolines, solids, silk organzas, and sheers (page 21)

Painting supplies (page 22)

Transfer and stencil supplies (page 21)

Stamping supplies (page 22)

THE BASICS

A map uses several important aspects of the elements of design: value, color, form, shape, line, space, and texture. However, lines and shapes are the heart of a map because they are fundamental to communicating the valuable information that brings a map to life, so this chapter focuses on techniques for making lines and shapes using various media.

Lines and shapes give a map meaning and beauty. They also create different feelings and perceptions. For instance, they can be angry, strong, delicate, anguished, and more. Close examination of the things around you exposes noteworthy discoveries about these elements that can be used in your work.

LINES AND SHAPES ON THE LANDSCAPE

Lines

Lines can be vertical, horizontal, diagonal, straight, curved, bent, angular, and free form.

Lines can represent streams, furrows, ridges, riverbanks, brooks, creeks, watercourses, estuaries, channels, straits, roads, paths, fences, streets, tracks, lanes, gateways, alleys, passages, walkways, sidewalks, trails, footbridges, gouges, grooves, gullies, gutters, raceways, routes, and runways.

Lines
Drawing by Dario McPhee

Shapes

Shapes can be circles, ovals, triangles, squares, rectangles, parallelograms, trapezoids, pentagons, hexagons, and octagons; they can be asymmetrical, irregular, and amorphous.

Shapes can represent buildings, huts, cabins, barns, castles, churches, temples, hovels, shacks, shanties, sheds, cottages, wells, benches, pavilions, stepping stones, ponds, lakes, trees, basins, lagoons, pools, garden patches, vegetation areas, meadows, fields, crop circles, pastures, patches of land, plots, tracts, bayous, coves, inlets, and sinkholes.

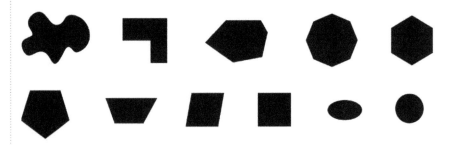

Shapes
Drawing by Dario McPhee

Techniques for Creating Lines and Shapes

FUSING

The smaller the element, the more likely I am to fuse it down. It is just a more practical technique than hand or machine appliqué for detailed work. As an added precaution, I secure these pieces to the background with free-motion stitches.

Before you start fusing, be sure to read the fusible web manufacturer's instructions. Prepare fabric for fusing by ironing the fusible web to the wrong side of the fabric. Cut out the shapes and iron/fuse them to the fabric background. To add a pop of detail, sew all around the fused fabric with contrasting thread.

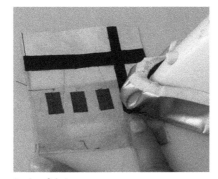
Fusing fabric

 TIP

Use a nonstick appliqué sheet or Silicone Release Paper to protect the ironing board when you are using fusible webs.

HAND STITCHING

The expressive nature of the hand-sewn stitch is a wonderful tool at your disposal. Why not try representing a thin line such as a path with a lovely hand-stitched line? Make the edge of a pond the same way. Try varying the length and width of the stitches for different effects.

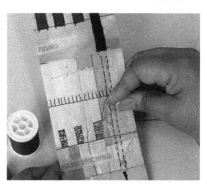
Hand-stitched lines and shapes

Fused lines and shapes

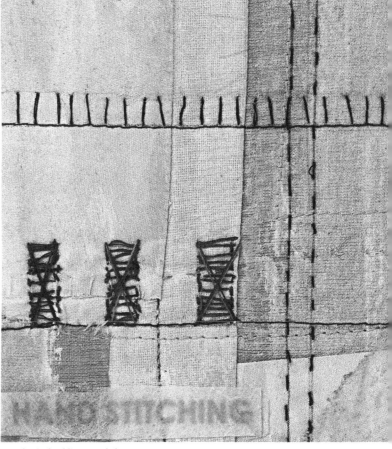
Hand-stitched lines and shapes

MACHINE STITCHING

Machine stitching is good for making lines and outlining shapes. Use a straight stitch or try out the decorative stitches on your sewing machine. I love using a simple satin stitch, adjusting the width for different results.

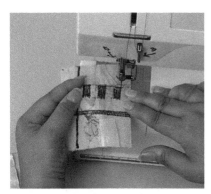

Machine-stitched lines and shapes

STAMPING

Make your own stamp or use everyday objects to create shapes and lines. Refer to Stamping Supplies (page 22) for a list of stamping objects and materials as a starting point. Stamping is an easy way to add detail to a map. Apply full-strength paint to the stamps using a foam brush and then press firmly onto the fabric.

Stamped shapes

Stamped lines

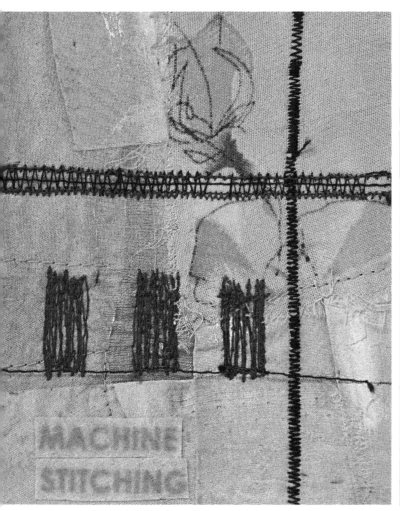

Machine-stitched lines and shapes

Stamped lines and shapes

APPLIQUÉ

Appliqué works well for larger shapes and lines. It adds a bit of depth to a map. I use it occasionally for large roads and landscape elements. Choose your favorite method of appliqué, whether by hand or machine. Finish machine-appliquéd elements by using zigzag or satin stitches of various widths or even raw-edge appliqué to secure the fabric pieces in place.

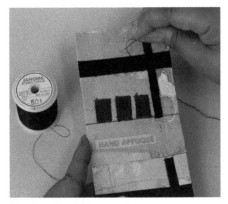

Hand-appliquéd lines and shapes

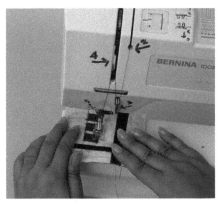

Machine-appliquéd lines and shapes

Hand-appliquéd lines and shapes

Machine-appliquéd lines and shapes

STENCILING

Stenciling sometimes works best if you are making a map from an existing drawing or map.

To make a stencil, use wax-free tracing paper to transfer the drawing onto poster board, cardstock, or another material appropriate for stencils. Consider scanning the drawing and printing it onto cardstock. Use a craft knife (such as an X-Acto) to cut out the stencil. This technique requires patience and careful cutting, but it is very effective. The holes that you cut are used to paint shapes on the background.

Select fabric paint that contrasts with the background, and make sure you have aligned the stencil properly before you begin painting. Use a small brush, sponge, or stencil brush to carefully paint the shapes. When the paint is dry to the touch, slowly peel away the stencil. Using a free-motion foot, outline the painted elements using thread.

Outlining the painted areas with machine stitching provides definition.

Refer to Adding Stones and Shadows (page 53) for another example of stenciling.

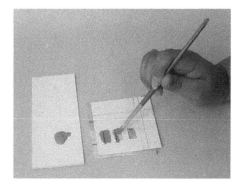

Paint shapes using stencil.

Stenciled shapes

Stenciled lines and shapes

MASKING

Almost any line or shape can be added to a map by taping off an area using painter's tape. You can opt for a clean, sharp edge or a torn edge. Remember to apply the paint parallel to the tape as much as possible to avoid having the paint seep under the tape. Allow the paint to dry and then carefully remove the tape. Sew an outline around the painted area.

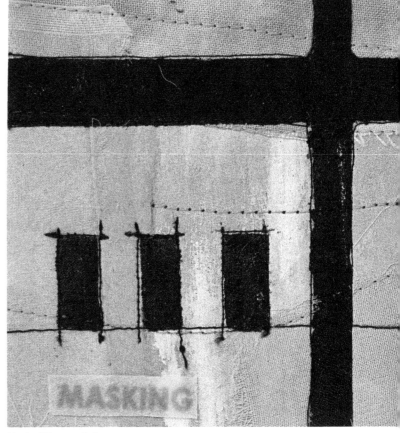

Masked areas on background

Masked lines and shapes

Overview of Techniques for Making Lines and Shapes

FUSING	Quick and effective way of applying lines and shapes, especially for small elements
HAND STITCHING	Gives a delicate and beautiful human-made quality to the surface
MACHINE STITCHING	Satin stitches are great for bold lines but can be hard to make expressive. Free-motion stitches provide an interesting texture.
STAMPING	Quick and simple way of adding repetitive lines and shapes
HAND APPLIQUÉ	Good way to apply larger lines and shapes. Hand appliqué stitches do not show, keeping the elements crisp and pure.
MACHINE APPLIQUÉ	Good way to apply larger lines and shapes, with the machine stitching that holds down the appliqué adding emphasis to these elements. You can control the degree of emphasis through the color you choose for the stitching.
STENCILING	Great way to make crisp lines or shapes
MASKING	Great way to make crisp lines or shapes

OTHER TECHNIQUES FOR MAKING LINES AND SHAPES

▪ reverse appliqué ▪ drawing with permanent pens ▪ beading ▪ couching

GALLERY OF LINES AND SHAPES

Detail of *Rattler Country*
(full quilt on page 80)

Fused lines and shapes

Detail of *City Grid IV*
(full quilt on pages 13 and 72)

Hand-appliquéd and masked lines, machine-stitched shapes

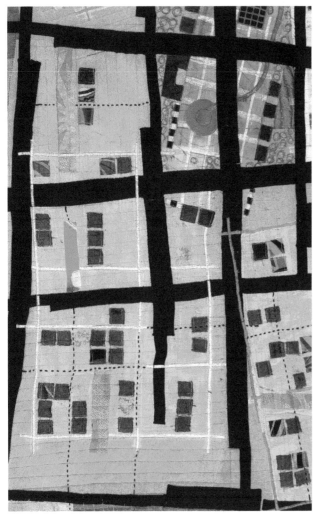

Detail of *City Grid III*
(full quilt on page 72)

**Combination of machine- and hand-stitched lines
as well as hand-appliquéd lines**

Detail of *African Burial Ground II*
(full quilt on page 76)

Machine-appliquéd lines

Detail of *The Economic Landscape*
(full quilt on page 77)

Stamped and fused lines and shapes

Detail of *The Economic Landscape*
(full quilt on page 77)

Fused shapes

Detail of *Labyrinth of the Hidden Goddess*
(full quilt on page 71)

Fused lines and shapes

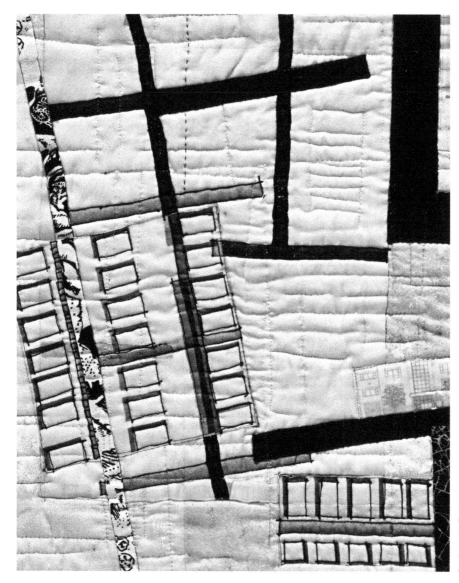

Detail of *ArchiTEXTural cARTography*
(full quilt on page 75)

Machine-stitched, masked, and hand-appliquéd lines

map haiku:
visual poetry

Now that you know how to create a background and add lines and shapes, you can put your newfound skills to use creating a map based on a haiku that you write.

Stretching yourself is an important part of growing as an artist. This chapter and the next two offer design exercises that are crafted for just this purpose. Poetry and art can go hand in hand, and the exercise in this chapter helps you create work in which each influences the other.

This exercise includes writing, design exploration, sketching, and construction using traditional quilting techniques such as hand and machine sewing. In addition, various mixed-media techniques such as painting, fusing, and collage are part of the process. It will be your map based on your haiku, so use the information that follows to make it your own.

WHAT IS A HAIKU?

Haiku is a minimalist style of poetry using a set number of syllables to create images in the mind or evoke emotion in the heart and soul. It is a great way to embrace simplicity and try your hand at a fiber-art map. There are four key concepts to focus on:

- simplicity - brevity - abstraction - elegance

WRITING THE HAIKU

This project can be started in a number of ways, but first and foremost, you need to draw from the poetic side of your brain. Write a haiku about a place, or better yet, write several. They can be based on an image in your mind, a photograph of a place that you find poetic, or even a scene in a movie. *Be sure the haiku conjures up two or three visual components of a map, such as a path, a park bench, and a stream. And make sure it includes a feeling or emotion.*

There are a number of interpretations of exactly what constitutes a haiku—I use a three-line stanza that has seventeen syllables using the following pattern:

Line 1: Five syllables *The / brook / and / foot / bridge*

Line 2: Seven syllables *con / nect / a / cross / yet / di / vide*

Line 3: Five syllables *the / here / and / the / there*

For this exercise, write your own haiku or select one of the following:

Far above the field / the elegant lines crossing / frame peaceful dwellings

Tracings on the land / grace monochromatic spaces / and serene dark places

Abandoned homes / the low walls remain / beside a lost road

Faded roads define / paths waiting for your return / city of broken hearts

A single gate marks / path through a clearing / across winter's field

The meandering road leads / to the old castle ruins / a journey's sad end

Down the country road / to a remote wishing well / I would catch daydreams

Ancient garden patch / sustained the villager / near the river's bend

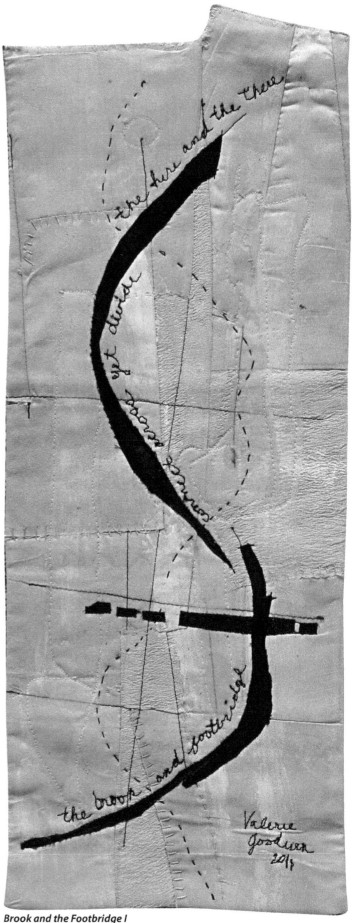

Brook and the Footbridge I
by Valerie S. Goodwin, 2011, 6½″ × 16″

MATERIALS

Basic equipment and supplies for sewing, cutting, and fusing (page 20)

Fabrics and stabilizers: crinolines, solids, silk organzas, and sheers (page 21)

Painting supplies (page 22)

Transfer and stencil supplies (page 21)

Stamping supplies (page 22)

THE DESIGN PROCESS

Now comes the design exploration! Select a few of your most compelling haiku. Remember it is important that each haiku contain two or three components of a map and that it express a feeling.

1. Get some 3″ × 5″ blank index cards and pens for sketching ideas. It is easier to explore ideas quickly using small drawings, which help you to focus on the overall idea and avoid getting bogged down in details.

Index cards and pens for sketching

2. Draw a few simple maps of the place. Incorporate simple lines, shapes, patterns, and textures. The map doesn't have to fill the entire index card—leave room on the card to write the haiku. Try to make each sketch simple, quick, and thoughtful.

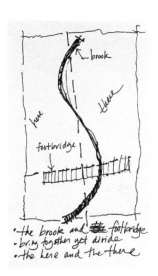
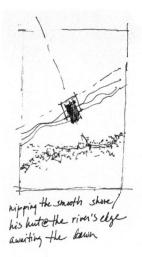
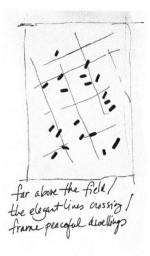

Sketches on index cards
Photos by C&T Publishing

 HINTS

Be abstract—avoid recognizable objects, letters, or numerals.

Be aware of the negative space—it helps to define the subject matter and the picture plane as well as keeping the eye moving around the composition.

Think about creating an uncomplicated and balanced composition; keep it simple.

The Vocabulary of Lines and Shapes

In the previous chapter you learned that lines and shapes are part of the map vocabulary. In a way, they are also a kind of handwriting and therefore have a style. You have your own distinct way of writing, so think about lines and shapes for this project in some of the following ways:

- They can begin thin, grow big, or run off the card.

- They can vary in length (short, medium, long) and may expand or contract in any form or direction.

- They can be straight, dashed, or curved; they can zigzag and twist; they can cross over, build on top of, weave under and through each other; and so on.

I generally use various black pens, but you might want to try charcoal or paint. Have fun and have no fear as you think about the following to get started:

- What in the haiku can be represented by lines?

- What in the haiku can be represented by shapes?

- What in the haiku can be represented by pattern?

- What in the haiku can be represented by texture?

- Could a line be a road or a gulley?

- Could a shape be a pond or a tree?

THE BACKGROUND

Selecting Fabrics

After you have some design sketches, it's time to start the background. Refer back to Background Music: The Landscape Layer (pages 23–27) as you read the next few sections.

The first or background layer is the base layer or the earth's surface. The subsequent layers make up the details of the map, such as roads, paths, landscaped areas, and buildings.

1. Select one of your index card sketches as the inspiration for this exercise. I chose the following haiku and sketch.

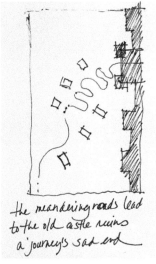

The meandering road leads / to the old castle ruins / a journey's sad end
Photo by C&T Publishing

2. Plan to make the haiku map quilt bigger than the index card sketch; 7″–8″ × 10″–11″ is a good size.

3. The background (the earth's surface) should convey a feeling of subtlety and richness. It is an abstract representation of a landscape; it is the backdrop and plays a supporting role so that the detail elements will stand out.

Pay careful attention to the fabric selection. I suggest using fabric that is solid or has a subtle texture or pattern.

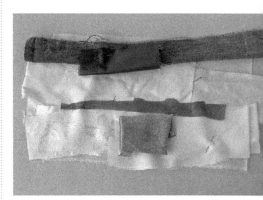

Fabric for map haiku: solids, hand dyes, and sumptuous kimono scraps

I chose a limited color palette because I felt that this design called for understatement and I wanted the lines and shapes on the land to tell most of the poetic story. I also thought about the feelings of sadness conveyed in my chosen haiku. In other words, fabric choice is an important part of being true to the poetry.

The Opaque Layer

1. Start with a piece of crinoline that is the size you want to make the map. Gather the fabric selections for the background and cut them into several pieces. The goal is to cover the crinoline with the fabric that will serve as the background to the map.

2. Using the sew-and-flip technique (see The Opaque Layer, Step 3, page 24), cover the crinoline with the fabric in a casual fashion. Don't overthink it. As you sew, try extending the machine stitching lines beyond the edges of some of the pieces. When you are finished, trim the fabrics to the edge of the crinoline.

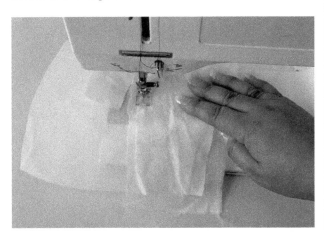

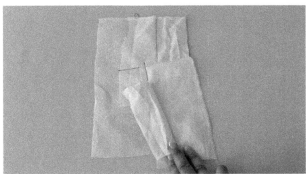

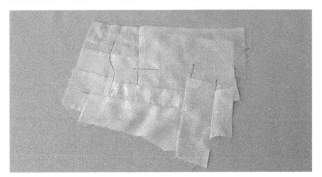

Sew and flip to attach fabrics to crinoline.

3. Add some hand stitching for texture and nuance. You will notice some areas where the raw edges of the fabric are exposed. Hand stitch the raw edges down (see Hand Stitching, page 31). I used a very simple embroidery stitch.

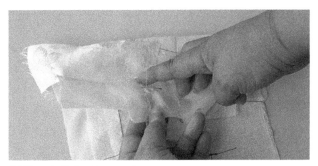

Add hand stitches to raw edges.

Have you ever looked at a patch of land from above and marveled at the beauty of the fine marks in the land? For this map, I focused on the textural quality created by lines that are sometimes seen etched in the landscape. To achieve that effect, I added a few hand-stitched lines across the fabric surface.

The Painted Layer

Add texture in a few selected areas using fabric paint or acrylic paint (see The Painted Layer, page 25).

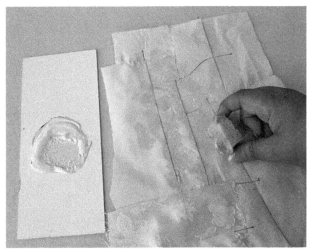

Add paint for interest and texture.

The Translucent Layer

Adding a few pieces of translucent fabrics will give the surface a watercolor effect. Silk organza, sheer drapery fabric with a subtle print, or even crinoline are recommended choices.

Prepare the fabric for fusing (see Fusing, page 31), cut it to size, and fuse it down. Have fun; you don't have to think too long and hard about this step. Applying this fabric across bordering fabrics helps to blend the colors and minimize abrupt changes in color. Be sure to sew around the edge of the fused piece with a sewing machine. Use an invisible thread or thread that is close in color to the sheer fabric if you want subtlety.

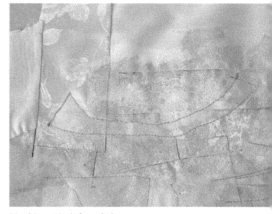

Machine stitch fused sheers.

The Map Details

Refer to Putting It on the Map: Techniques to Create Lines and Shapes (page 28) for the techniques to add the map elements from your haiku. Remember that like a haiku, this map is about creating a work of art that is simple and understated, so keep the details at a minimum. My haiku map includes a road, a few buildings, and the castle on the right edge of the map.

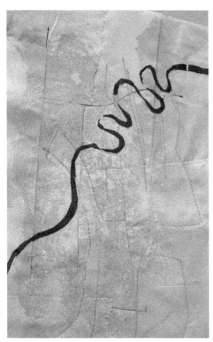

Road fused to background

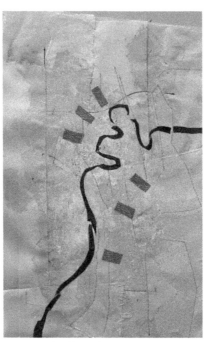

Roads and buildings fused to background

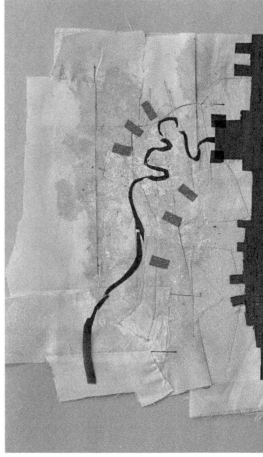

All the map elements fused to background

Finishing

When you are pleased with your map, it is time to finish it off. Carefully press the finished map (the quilt top). Prepare the quilt sandwich by layering the quilt back, wrong side up, followed by a thin piece of batting, and topping it off with the quilt top, face up. Baste the layers together. For an art map this size I use only a few quilting stitches by machine. In this case I tried to outline some of the textured areas on the surface.

Using free-motion quilting, write the haiku on the front surface of the quilt.

Trim and finish the edges using your preferred method.

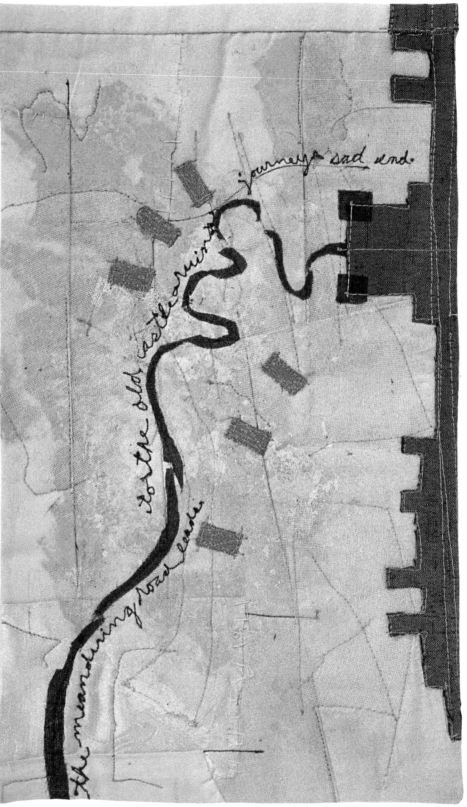

Meandering Road I by Valerie S. Goodwin, 2012, 7″ × 11″

GALLERY

I made some of the following fiber maps; others were made by workshop students. I hope these examples inspire you to make your own.

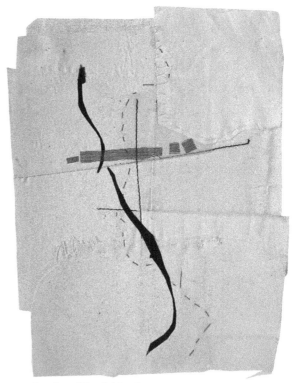

Brook and Footbridge II
by Valerie S. Goodwin, 2010, 5″ × 7″

The brook and footbridge / connect across yet divide / the here and the there

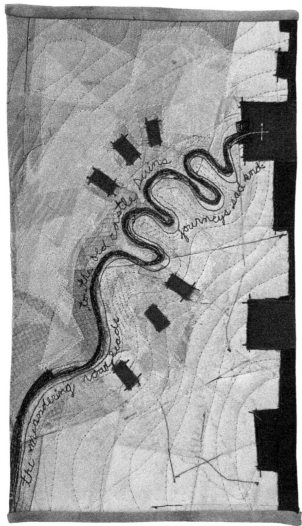

Meandering Road II
by Valerie S. Goodwin, 2012, 7″ × 11″

The meandering road leads / to the old castle ruins / a journey's sad end

Ancient Garden Patch
by Valerie S. Goodwin, 2010, 3″ × 5″

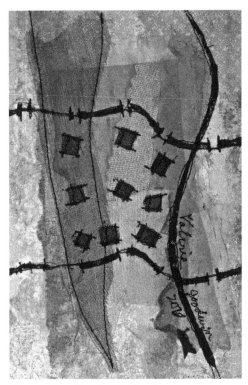

Elegant Lines Crossing the Land
by Valerie S. Goodwin, 2010, 3″ × 5″

Far above the field / the elegant lines crossing /
frame peaceful dwellings
Photo by Valerie S. Goodwin

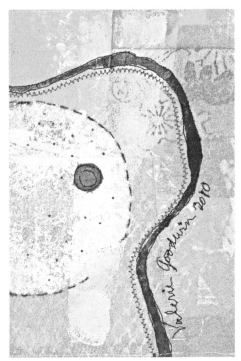

Wishing Well
by Valerie S. Goodwin, 2010, 3″ × 5″

Down the country road / to a remote wishing well /
I would catch daydreams
Photo by Valerie S. Goodwin

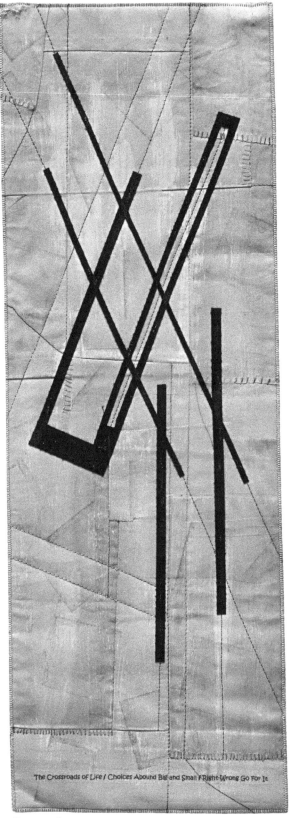

Crossroads
by Linda M. Cole, 2012, 6½″ × 18″

The crossroads of life / choices abound
big and small / right-wrong go for it

Translucent Fields
by Suanne Summers, 2011, 11″ × 16″

Translucent fields / beneath stalks of rushing wheat / pure in their intent

435 Signal Hill Road
by Julie Rivera, 2012, 6″ × 17½″

Force divides garden and open field

Serene Dark Places
by Jo P. Griffith, 2012, 13½″ × 17¾″

Tracings on the land / grace monochromatic spaces / and serene dark places

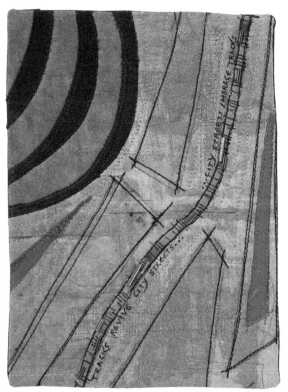

Urban Renewal
by Deborah Langsam, 2012, 5″ × 7″

Tracks revive city streets / city streets embrace tracks

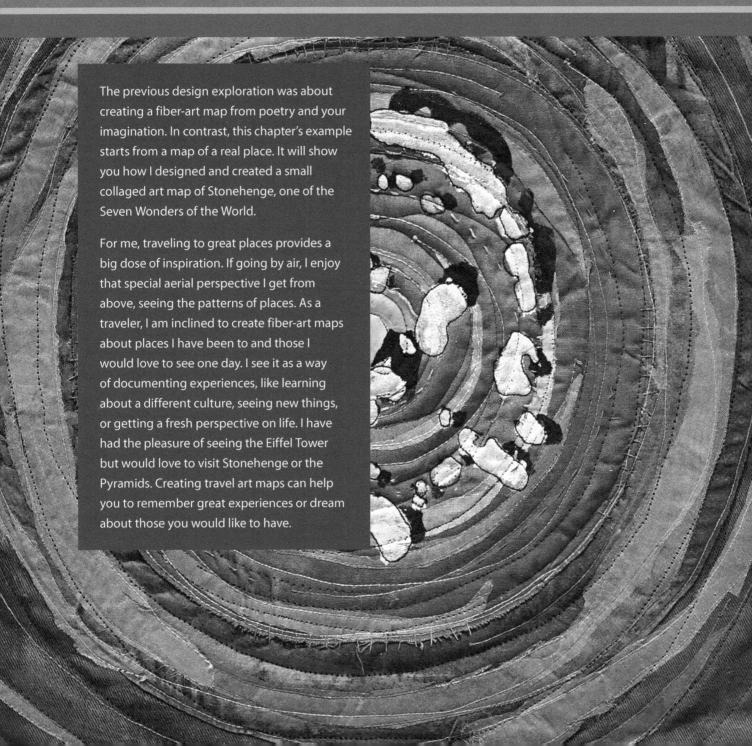

fiber-art
travel maps

The previous design exploration was about creating a fiber-art map from poetry and your imagination. In contrast, this chapter's example starts from a map of a real place. It will show you how I designed and created a small collaged art map of Stonehenge, one of the Seven Wonders of the World.

For me, traveling to great places provides a big dose of inspiration. If going by air, I enjoy that special aerial perspective I get from above, seeing the patterns of places. As a traveler, I am inclined to create fiber-art maps about places I have been to and those I would love to see one day. I see it as a way of documenting experiences, like learning about a different culture, seeing new things, or getting a fresh perspective on life. I have had the pleasure of seeing the Eiffel Tower but would love to visit Stonehenge or the Pyramids. Creating travel art maps can help you to remember great experiences or dream about those you would like to have.

This chapter will show you how I designed and created a small collaged art map of a real place.

I invite you to work along with me and make your own Stonehenge or to apply the same principles and techniques to a destination of your choice.

It is important to think about what you want to express in a travel map. For this exploration, the aim is to convey the feeling of a strong center defined by a circular arrangement of forms (the stones). The implied concentric circles of the site can be thought of as shapes and lines. When completed, shape, color, and line will come together to create a very striking map of this ancient and mysterious prehistoric monument and express the strong center and circular dynamic. A view from the top and a powerful side view will work well together to this end.

Necropolis **by Valerie S. Goodwin, 2008, 11″ × 11¾″**

WHERE TO FIND MAPS

There are many sources for maps. As with almost everything these days, the Internet is a good source for a map of the place you are interested in creating. It will be helpful if you can locate a source that has multiple views of a site, such as line drawings, photos, and aerial views of the location. Occasionally, you may find a useful tourist map or an architectural site plan of the place. Below is a short list of resources:

Google Maps: www.maps.google.com

Mappery: www.mappery.com

Bing Maps: www.bing.com/maps

Your local city or county geographic information system (GIS) website

U.S. Geological Survey topographic maps: www.usgsquads.com > MapFinder

Park service maps

Charts used by boaters

MATERIALS

Basic equipment and supplies for sewing, cutting, and fusing (page 20)

Fabrics and stabilizers: crinolines, solids, organzas, and sheers (page 21)

Painting supplies (page 22)

Transfer and stencil supplies (page 21)

Stamping supplies (page 22)

NOTE

For the concentric circles:

° *Circle 1 has a radius of 5½".*

° *Circle 2 has a radius of 4".*

° *Circle 3 has a radius of 2½".*

° *Circle 4 has a radius of ¾".*

CREATING A PATTERN

The first step was to locate a map of Stonehenge that clearly shows the outline of the main shapes as well as an aerial view. I printed out the aerial view at the needed scale and traced off the stones, the shadows, and the main shape of the site. The templates or patterns for a project such as this can be traced by hand or electronically; see Tips (below). Enlarge or reduce the drawing to about 11″ × 17″.

I made patterns such as those you see below with four separate drawings: the concentric circles, the shadows, the stones, and a combined drawing with the side view at the top. I left a few inches at the top to draw a simple outline of the side view of Stonehenge.

TIPS

Use a lightbox or a large window to help make a tracing if you are working by hand.

Sometimes switching the colors and line weights of the pen or pencil can be helpful in designating different types of information.

Simplify the information you decide to trace. You can always add detail later on.

For the more technically inclined, you can use a vector-based software such as CorelDraw, Photoshop, or AutoCAD by importing the aerial image and creating a digital tracing that is a simplified version of the site.

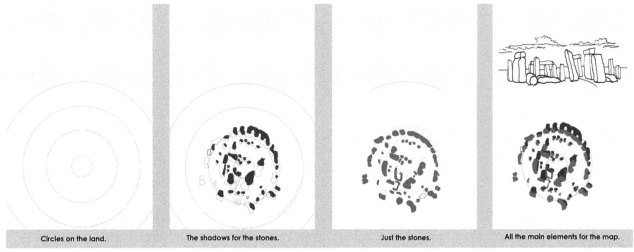

Circles on the land.   The shadows for the stones.   Just the stones.   All the main elements for the map.

Stonehenge drawings by author

CREATING THE BACKGROUND LAYER

To set up the base layer, I started with a 12″ × 18″ piece of crinoline (just a bit bigger than the finished size of 11″ × 17″).

Let's think about value. To make the map elements stand out, I decided on the following:

- The shadows will be darkest.

- The stones will be of medium value.

- The concentric circles on the land will either alternate in value or gradually change from a dark value to a light one as they move toward the center.

The Concentric Circles

For a painterly effect, I used solid fabrics (commercial and hand dyed). I cut the darkest fabric into a 12″ × 12″ square and stitched it to the crinoline, with the bottom edge aligned with the edge of the crinoline. The stitching formed a cross centered on the 12″ × 12″ fabric to establish the center point of the square so the centers of the concentric circles could be aligned properly.

Using the dimensions of the circles from the drawing, I cut four different pieces of fabric and raw-edge appliquéd them (see Appliqué, page 33) to the dark base. Then I added hand stitching for texture.

Hand stitching

After preparing white organza for fusing (see Fusing, page 31), I cut a series of arcs, all based on the same center point, and ironed them to the background. Then I stitched down the edges of the organza by machine.

Fusing silk organza arcs to fabric surface

Machine stitching fused arcs in place

For added embellishment, I added hand- and machine-stitched concentric circles to the surface. Circular strokes of paint added a sense of energy and life.

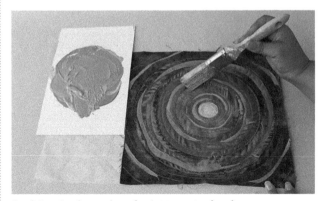

Applying circular strokes of paint to parts of surface

ADDING STONES AND SHADOWS

I used stencils to paint the stones and shadows. First I made a few photocopies of the template by printing it onto 11″ × 17″ cardstock. I used a craft knife (such as an X-Acto) to cut out a stencil of just the stones and then did the same on a second piece of cardstock for just the shadows.

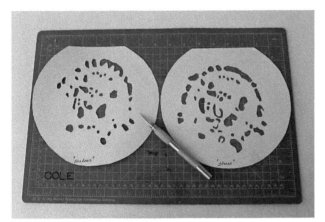

Stencils for stones and shadows

The stenciling started with the shadows. I used dark fabric paint to contrast with the background surface. It's important to make sure the stencil is properly aligned with the center point before beginning. I used a stencil brush to add the shadows. After the paint was dry, I outlined the shadows with free-motion stitching using dark thread.

Adding shadows using stencil

I repeated the same process for the stones with paint chosen to contrast with the background and the shadows. I recommend the contrasting paint be a few steps lighter in value than the shadows. Then I outlined each stone with free-motion stitching.

Adding stones using stencil

Free-motion stitching around each stone for definition

ADDING CONTEXT

Context is a great way to tell the story of a place. In this case that would certainly be the majestic stones. I found a great copyright-free image to use for the context drawing at the top of the map. In essence, the aerial view of the earth's surface has a double reading in the composition. The bottom portion of the map should read as the ground on which the stones sit. Looking at the completed piece (page 56) for reference, you will see the aerial view of the site as the dominant part of the composition. However, the way the side view of Stonehenge is placed at the top edge of the site, the aerial view at this line starts to double as the ground that supports the stones.

To begin this part of the map, I added a piece of fabric about 5″ × 12″ to the top of the map for the sky. I chose a fabric with a sky pattern and stitched it in place with several wavy horizontal lines.

Adding sky fabric

Next, I used paint to create a dark area on the land for the stones to sit in profile (sheer fabric would also work well). The dark area helps anchor the stones and makes them stand out against the land.

Creating dark area for stones

I traced the copyright-free image of the stones in profile on organza, using a thin- to medium-tipped permanent, waterproof archival pen.

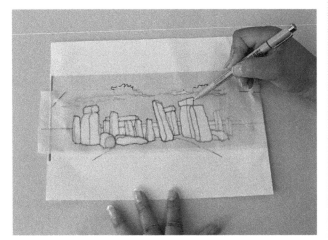

Tracing stones onto organza using permanent pens

To make the drawing opaque, I fused a piece of very light fabric to the back of the tracing. With a light-colored acrylic ink, I gave the stone a sense of form and shadow. For a bit more definition, I used a watercolor pencil to finish the drawing. When dry, I heat set it with an iron.

Fusing light-colored fabric to back of organza

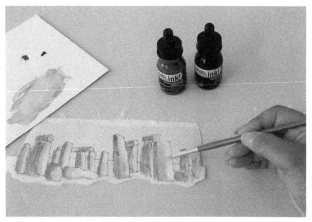

Adding form to stones using acrylic ink

Adding definition with watercolor pencil

I ironed fusible web to the back of the light fabric, cut out the image, and placed it at the top of the piece. When I was satisfied with the placement, I ironed it down and stitched around the edges with contrasting thread. I repeated this process for each stone and shadow. Then I finished the quilt top as described in Finishing (page 45).

Completed fiber-art travel map of Stonehenge

FOR YOUR CONSIDERATION

When making a fiber-art map, the color palette of the fabric, paint, and thread does not have to be realistic. In fact, using an abstract selection of colors may yield a more interesting work of art. For example, you might try a monochromatic scheme, such as all shades of purple. Keep in mind that colors are often selected to create emotional effect, but whatever your color choices are, value is extremely important, and you generally need to include a range from dark to light.

You are the designer. Do you want a dramatic feeling for the sky? Should it reflect sunrise, sunset, or an afternoon storm? You decide. If you make your own version of Stonehenge, how might you change the sizes and place-ment of the concentric circles? Think about how you might suggest a sense of power by changing the width and progression of the circles.

You can finish small fiber-art maps using traditional quiltmaking tech-niques, or you can mat the quilt top and set it a beautiful frame.

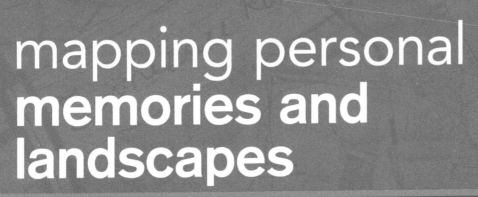

mapping personal
memories and
landscapes

STARTING PLACES

Having a concept behind your work is important. In my art, I strive to create a connection between the viewer and what I have seen and experienced. Sometimes inspiration comes from memories, random doodling, images, or almost anything around me. The idea, crystallized into words, may emerge at the beginning or coalesce as I move forward in the design. Either way, I have found that a clear direction or road map is essential if I want the design to have an intention.

For quite a long time, I have had the idea of doing a fiber-art map that celebrates two places that were part of my formative years. They were two cherished locations in Tuscumbia and Sheffield, Alabama, where my grandparents lived. My personal memories of these places remain fondly embedded in my mind. At times, there is a sense of these places' being very real, yet at other moments, they seem very abstract and dreamlike. As a follow-up to the two previous chapters, I think it is fitting to document making a fiber map based on something real and rooted in memory. You may have similar memories of a place in your childhood that could serve as a starting point for your own fiber-art map.

Places where my grandparents lived when I was a child

This chapter is about providing a glimpse into following an idea from conception to completion. The focus will be on the design process, not technique. Consider the following pages as a kind of visual diary about the evolution of one of my works.

WORDS AND MEMORIES

"Text me!" This is what I said to my sisters Stacy and Sylvia, as I tried to put together memories of visiting my grandparents. I am the eldest of four sisters who grew up in Connecticut and traveled south each summer with much joy and anticipation. As I awaited their texts throughout the morning, I knew their thoughts would be useful. Below are some of the words they shared with me on my cell phone:

- small-town living   - wide-open spaces   - church
- "Sweet Hour of Prayer" (a classic gospel song)
- sitting and swinging on the porch   - warm summers
- loud crickets   - fireflies   - homemade ice cream
- lots of visitors   - connection to the community
- visiting relatives   - crops   - living by the highway
- everything made from scratch
- *Lawrence Welk* (our maternal grandfather's Saturday night TV show)

As I ran through the words and phrases in my brain, I knew it would be important to let the actual words become part of the quilt, so I decided to incorporate text into the map. The words would become one of the details appreciated by the viewer on close inspection of the design. I have used text in other work when I felt words would help convey important feelings (for example, *The Economic Landscape*, page 77, and *African Burial Ground II*, page 76), as many artists have to convey ideas about their personal life.

COLLECTING THE IMAGES

Everyday life can get quite busy, making it difficult to stop and document family memories. While making this quilt, I became a hunter-gatherer of old family photographs. This process became very meaningful to me as it conjured up more memories and led me to connect with family members I had not spoken with in a while, especially those that have become the keepers of treasured, timeworn family photographs. I collaged the words and the family images on a wall in my studio for inspiration. This display became useful reference throughout the design process.

Collage of memory words and family images

COLLECTING THE REFERENCE MAPS

As discussed in Fiber-Art Travel Maps (page 49), there are many ways to find maps. I had started collecting a few maps of the area years ago and stored them on my computer hard drive. These maps were useful, but they were not old enough to depict what was there when I visited as a child. As a result, I altered the maps to reflect what I could remember.

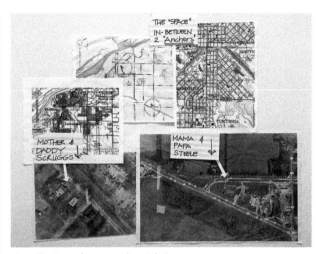

My collection of maps and aerial views

As I studied the maps, I began to see my grandparents' environment in a different way. I remembered the local trips between the homes. I became aware of the journey as a transition between places with different characteristics. As a result, I started to compare and contrast the two places.

My maternal grandparents lived in a rural environment, where the houses had plenty of space between them. The house was set slightly up a red clay hill, anchoring a wedge-shaped piece of land. Imagine country living beside a southern highway with a cornfield in the backyard. Embracing this idyllic rural setting was the sense of community, despite the distance between the houses in this area.

My paternal grandparents lived in a more dense area, with streets based on a grid. Right across the street from their house was a window-manufacturing plant, whose presence seemed out of scale to the modest homes around it. This was something I took for granted back then, but in hindsight I realize how unusual it was. I am now very aware that these grandparents lived on the border between housing and a small industrial zone. Apart from this context, the great part about their living here was that the nearest relative was just a few houses down the way. I remember all the visitors and times spent sitting on the porch and the treasured garden bench in the front yard. It was a special place to visit, filled with love and pride.

DESIGN SKETCHES

I began moving forward with the design sketches knowing that I wanted to use three maps:

- The site where my maternal grandparents lived

- The site where my paternal grandparents lived

- The route between the two

I knew I needed to revise and augment the maps I had collected. For this project, I worked by hand and on the computer.

To filter out the unimportant details I saw in the map of the area between the two homes, I decided to make a simplified sketch. Placing a piece of tracing paper on top of the map, I made a sketch of the area, highlighting the route with a dark line.

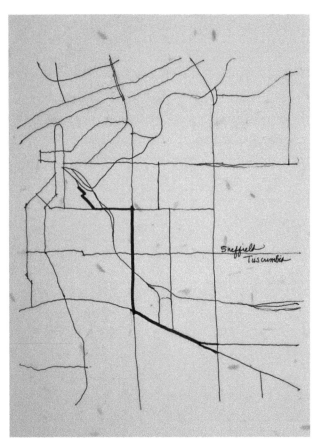

Simplified sketch of the route between my grandparents' homes
Photo by C&T Publishing

After making this simple drawing, I scanned it to create an image file. After some experimentation, I placed an image file of a map of one grandparents' site above it and the other one right below. When satisfied with the arrangement, I saved it and printed this design out to create another tracing.

Composite image of three maps made using image-editing software with added photos of my grandparents
Image by Valerie S. Goodwin

Design sketch with all three maps
Photo by C&T Publishing

Design sketch tweaked using image-editing software

Sometimes I enjoy going back and forth between using hand sketches and my image-editing software to explore design ideas. At times, I find this exercise a great way to play with color and contrast. It can also be a good way to tweak the design without committing myself to hours of redrawing. Even though I may spend time doing this, I always allow my work to evolve as I go along.

As I prepared a sketch of all three areas, I thought about the possible connections between the lines and shapes. I was interested to see how the two larger-scale maps worked with the smaller-scale map of the route. I made a combined design sketch using my image-editing software.

PREP WORK

The next step was selecting fabric and colors that represented several ideas:

- The red clay earth in Alabama

- The earthy quality of the people

- The green and fertile nature of the land

- The Tennessee River, a powerful landmark of the area

- Using light, medium, and dark fabric to provide contrast and develop a subtle gradation of color from the top to the bottom of the map

Having found the fabric to reflect these goals, I moved on to prep work. I traced the main lines and shapes onto crinoline to make it easier to transfer this information to the fabric later on. I used dark permanent pens so the traced lines could be seen on both sides of the crinoline.

Auditioning fabric
Photo by C&T Publishing

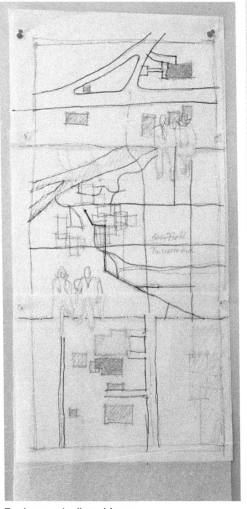

Tracing on crinoline with map underneath

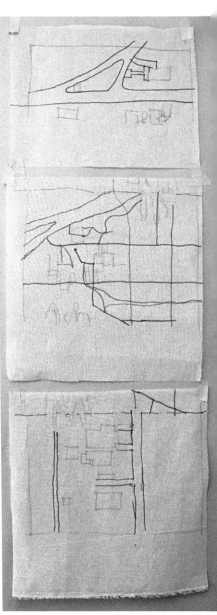

Sections of crinoline with traced lines and shapes

CREATING THE BACKGROUND LAYER

Using some of the methods described in Background Music: The Landscape Layer (page 23), I began to sew fabric to the crinoline. I tried to create a gradation of color to identify the three map zones, going from lighter to darker fabrics vertically. Another goal was to make the top map more organic, the middle one rectilinear, and the bottom one more vertical. Refer to More Backgrounds (page 27) for examples of creating different effects on the background layer of a fiber-art map.

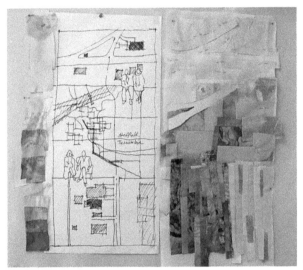

Adding first layer of fabric to crinoline base

After completely covering the crinoline with the first layer of fabric, I added hand stitching and paint to certain areas. The direction of the stitching and the paint strokes reinforced the geometric ideas I wanted to represent: organic, rectilinear, and vertical.

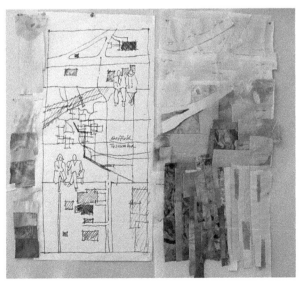

Painted and hand-stitched background

To create a watercolor effect and to add understated complexity, I began to add sheer fabric to the surface (see The Translucent Layer, page 25).

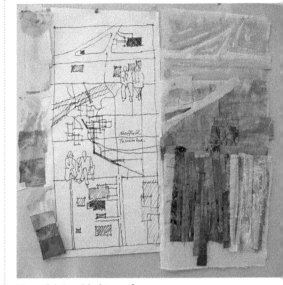

Sheer fabric added to surface

I created marks in the land by adding machine stitching in contrasting thread, at the same time using the stitching to secure any loose edges of fabric. In addition, I carefully chose the shapes and angles of these lines to work with the geometrical language of each section of the map.

Machine stitching added to surface

PUTTING IT ON THE MAP

After finishing the earth's surface, I located key lines and shapes, such as streets, by looking at the reverse side of the quilt. As you recall, I had made a tracing on top of the crinoline. The traced lines were dark enough to also appear on the flip side of the crinoline. At this point the previously drawn lines became very useful. I used them to locate the streets near my paternal grandparents' home. I machine stitched this information from the back, using thread that would stand out on the front. In the photo to the right, you can see the streets highlighted with white paint; a similar process worked well in other sections of the map.

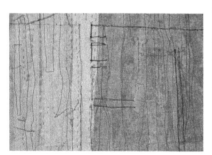

Flip side of crinoline showing black lines representing streets

Front side of quilt with black lines stitched using lines on crinoline

Front side of quilt with roads highlighted using white paint

I worked on the three maps as separate parts. This approach gave me control over each section. In addition, it gave me time to reflect on how I would join them visually and structurally.

I kept the top map, the area where my maternal grandparents lived, light in value. I used soft colors that had the sense of being floral, light, and airy. Perhaps my memories of learning to sew and my grandmother's flower beds were on my mind.

Top section of map in process

The middle portion of the map represented the place "in between" the two destinations. I remember going from open lands to more developed areas. The decision to use a loose rectilinear pattern on the background was related to the fact that this area was more grid-like.

Another key part of this map was the mighty Tennessee River and the bridge that spanned it. These elements were the important landmarks. Traveling across the bridge to the other side of the river was always a treat for me as a child. My paternal grandparents' home was not far from the river, nestled against a mix of manufacturing industries.

Middle section of map in process

The bottom section of the map was intentionally darker in value to anchor the bottom of the quilt. This choice also reflects the fact that these grandparents lived on the edge of a manufacturing zone. I decided to emphasize verticality to give this portion of the work a sense of movement beyond the edge.

Despite being near an industrial zone, the feeling of a welcoming small town was apparent. Look closely and you can see where I started to use the memory words discussed at the beginning of this chapter. More paint and sheer fabric were needed to lighten up the feeling of this zone. That concern would be addressed as I completed the quilt.

Bottom section of map in process

REACHING FOR THE FINISH LINE

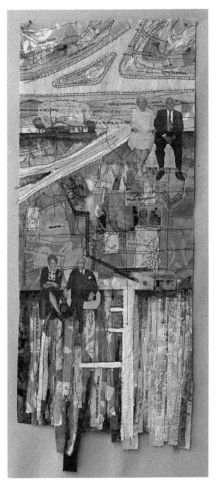

Paint added to make distinction between maps

When satisfied with each separate map, I sewed them together. To emphasize that these were distinct maps, I added paint at the top section of each. My technique was to let the paint gradually fade away and become part of the background. Notice that at some points the sections merge and at others they overlap—showing that these maps are all very connected.

My next task was to add the site details as well as the photographs of each home and my grandparents. I printed these images onto inkjet fabric, added fusible web to the back, and placed them in the spots I had designated in my initial sketches.

Images printed on fabric prepared for inkjet printing

I named the completed piece *Landscapes of Legacy*. Although this is a finished work, I also realize that this particular work has special qualities that might lead one day to another quilt. It may even become part of a series.

As I make art, I realize that many times one thing leads to another. Writing this chapter and making this piece has been quite a journey, and I don't think I am done with this subject matter. I know that many memory maps hang out there in my mind. I am excited by this idea and want to create other maps about my memories. Hopefully, after reading about the evolution of this piece, you will make your own memory-based fiber-art maps.

Landscapes of Legacy
by Valerie S. Goodwin,
2012, 18″ × 36″

gallery of work
by the author

This chapter is dedicated to showing examples of my fiber-art work. It includes some of my most recent work as well as some earlier pieces. Its purpose is to let you look at my art as a whole and perhaps reflect on changes in style, content, and technique over time.

The work I do today has evolved since 1998, when I made my first traditional quilt. A variety of themes and a range of techniques led to the first fiber-art map I made in 2001, called *City Grid II*. Looking at it today, I realize this quilt represents a breakthrough and records the point when I started to use fabric collage. From that period forward, I think I was able to create work that is recognizable as mine. I hope you will appreciate what you see in this chapter as part of my desire to make work that reflects an ongoing dialogue between maps, quilting, and *the architectural way of designing*.

City Grid II
by Valerie S. Goodwin
2001, 39″ × 46″
in the private collection
of Peter Stone
Photo by Richard Brunck

This quilt reflects on the interactive patterns and densities in a city grid and is the first fiber-art map in which I was able to be expressive using fabric collage.

Riverside Settlement
by Valerie S. Goodwin
2003, 38″ × 50″
in the private collection
of Sally and Mitch Seeley
Photo by Richard Brunck

Riverside Settlement recalls an ancient
network of interior and exterior places
along a river's edge. This quilt is important
to me because it was my first work to be
juried into an extremely competitive art
quilt venue.

Villa Rotunda
by Valerie S. Goodwin
2003, 12″ × 12″

Villa Rotunda is a map quilt based
on a real place. It is a site plan of a
Renaissance villa in northern Italy,
designed Andrea Palladio, a famous
sixteenth-century architect.

Labyrinth of the Hidden Goddess
by Valerie S. Goodwin
2005, 23″ × 35″
in the private collection
of Deborah LaGrasse

A map of a prehistoric goddess temple
inspired this piece. It is one of the first
maps in which I used layers of sheer fabric
and paint to achieve a painterly quality.

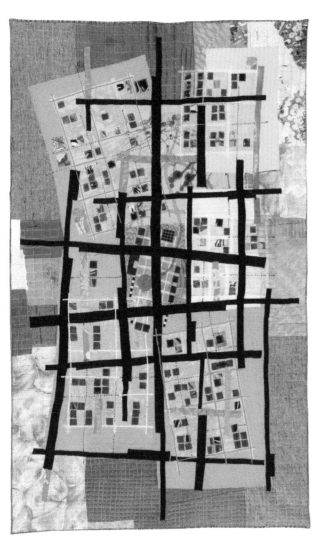

City Grid III
by Valerie S. Goodwin
2007, 32" × 44"
Photo by Richard Brunck

Improvisation was a key process in the creation of this work. As I made a series of small, unrelated maps, I thought about how city patterns layer and overlap. In response to this idea, I merged them to create a larger work. To unify the underlying patterns, I applied a more dominant grid of streets across the surface.

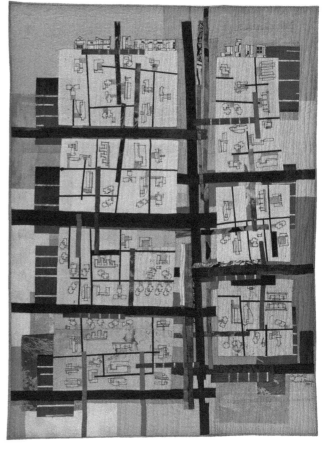

City Grid IV
by Valerie S. Goodwin
2007, 39" × 46"
Photo by Richard Brunck

A rigid system of organization is the focus of this piece about an imaginary place. As an experiment with multiple views in one work, some of the details of the map are represented as if seen from above while others offer a side view.

Place of Happy Accidents
by Valerie S. Goodwin
2008, 9" × 12¼"
in the private collection
of Joan Hughes

The title of this piece says it all—this map
composition was totally improvised. For me,
it represents what can happen when you
embrace accidental clues about how artwork
can evolve without any preconceived plan.

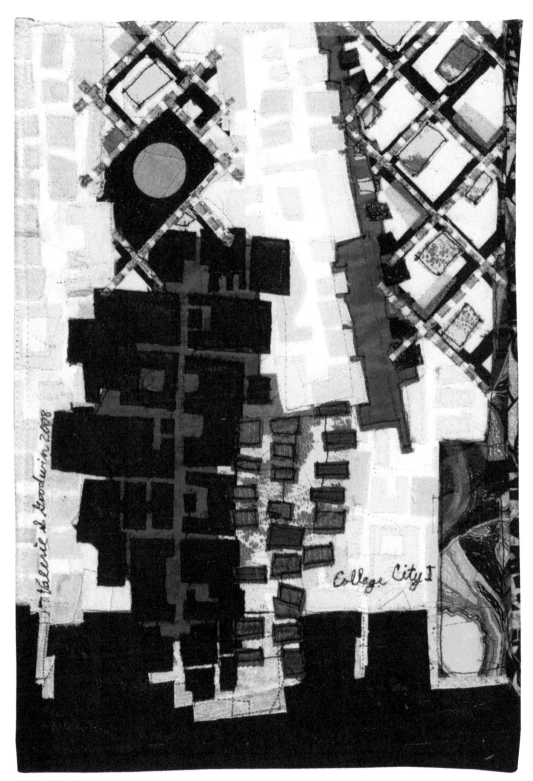

Collage City I
by Valerie S. Goodwin
2008, 9" × 12¼"
Photo by Richard Brunck

Collage City I was made as part of a series of
small studies to test ideas for larger work. It
juxtaposes various imaginary city maps and
collages them into one composition.

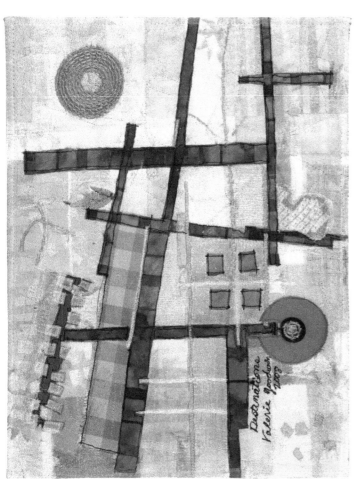
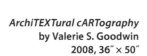

Destinations
by Valerie S. Goodwin
2008, 9″ × 12¼″
in the private collection
of Mary McBride
Photo by Richard Brunck

A small study of an imaginary map
with a focus on the use of nodes
and ending points.

ArchiTEXTural cARTography
by Valerie S. Goodwin
2008, 36″ × 50″

ArchiTEXTural cARTography is an
invented map. It uses a rectilinear grid
to play with the idea of roads that may
not connect and hierarchical elements
that play off each other.

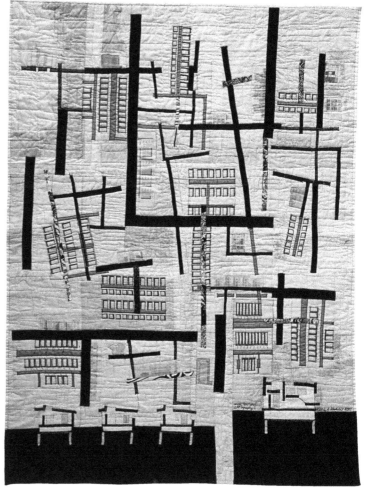

African Burial Ground II
by Valerie S. Goodwin
2009, 32″ × 44″

Fiber-art maps can tell a powerful story. The African Burial Ground, a real place in our country's history and now a national monument, served as the inspiration for this work. The previously forgotten and hidden life of African slaves living in Lower Manhattan during Colonial times spoke to me as a vehicle for artistic examination.

The Economic Landscape
by Valerie S. Goodwin
2009, 54″ × 32″

The design impetus for this work was
the economic meltdown of 2008. The
resulting fragmenting of our financial
landscape is portrayed using expressive
lines, shapes, and text.

Lay of the Land II
by Valerie S. Goodwin
2010, 7′0″ × 4′6″
in the private collection of Jack Walsh
Photo by Richard Brunck

The quilt, a triptych, is a commission wherein I used a
technique known as the composite drawing as a way to
interweave graphic elements such as aerial views, plans,
sections, and elevations in a cohesive and creative way. It
was inspired by Watkins Glen, New York, its surrounding
areas, and the site of a cottage owned by the client who
commissioned the work. I was struck by the geography, the
impact of the water features of the area, the artifacts, and
the natural beauty of the site surrounding the cottage. My
goal was to map a visual narrative of the architectural and
geographic imprint of the landscape of the area.

A Tale of Two Campuses
by Valerie S. Goodwin
2010, 4´ × 5´
in the private collection
of Al and Johan Hagaman
Photo by Richard Brunck

The line that marks the Tallahassee Railroad represents the cultural, economic, and historical divisions in our city. To many, this demarcation represents the differences from one side of the track to the other. This piece maps these differences between two campuses in my hometown: Florida A&M University and Florida State University. It offers a compelling story, weaving together architectural plans, maps, and digital images.

Rattler Country
by Valerie S. Goodwin
2012, 24″ × 48″

The campus where I teach
architecture is the subject
matter for this piece. This
site is also included, but at a
smaller scale, in *A Tale of Two
Campuses* (page 79).

Scattered Archaeologies II
by Valerie S. Goodwin
2012, 40½˝ × 26½˝
Photo by Ken Sharpe

This piece is derived from the organic language of the lines
on a map of an Iron Age settlement. Architectural remnants
such as a wall, columns, and buildings appear to move
around the picture plane. These elements are grounded at
the bottom with an image of the site at the base of the quilt.
After making this piece, I was inspired to write this haiku:

Scattered ruins / melancholy evidence / of distant glories.

gallery of work
by students

As I mentioned in the acknowledgments at the beginning of the book, the great work done by artists and quilters who have taken my workshops over the years has been important to me. This chapter is about showcasing that art. In addition, this section includes the creative work done by my architecture students who took a course from me about making fiber-art maps related to architecture. The work of these students has affected me as a teacher and an artist, and this chapter is devoted to letting you experience the creativity and craftsmanship I have seen from these students.

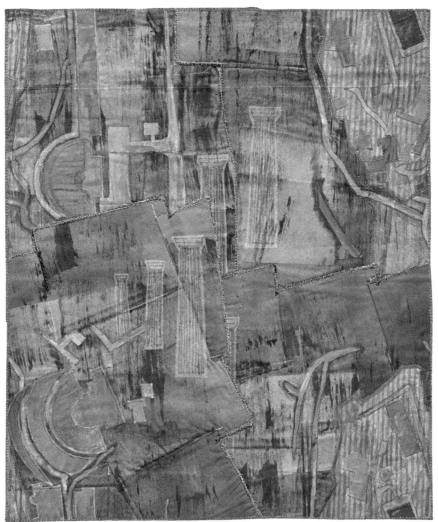

Atlantis
by Barbara Bushey
2011, 15″ × 18″

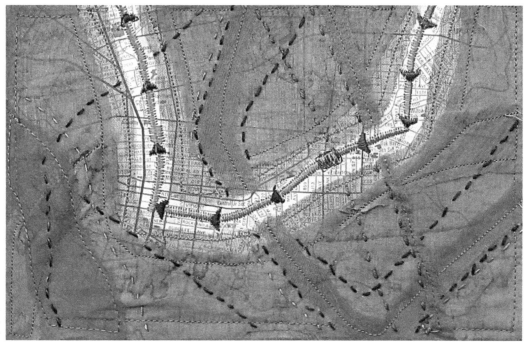

Going to Tea
by Kristin Rohr
2008, 6″ × 4″

A   B   C

1

2

3

4

D　　　　　　　　　　　E

Nolli Patchwork
2011, 80″ × 48″ (each panel 16″ × 12″)

A1	B1	C1	D1	E1
A2	B2	C2	D2	E2
A3	B3	C3	D3	E3
A4	B4	C4	D4	E4

Dezmond D. Ardis (D4)

Matthew D. Babbitt (D2)

Adam Chambers (A1)

James C. Eisele (B1)

Andrea Gallardo-Runk (D1)

Valerie S. Goodwin (E4)

Jody Ann James (C1)

Nicholas Kirkland (B3)

Susan Lee Marston (E1)

Garth McIntosh (A3)

Dario McPhee (A2)

Jerome L. Miller II (A4)

Jamaal Newbold (C3)

Miren P. Patel (B4)

Andrina Powell (B2)

Esther Roger (C2)

Jennifer I. Stewart (D3)

Millicent M. Swift (C4)

Lé Taj Tinker (E2)

Troy K. M. Williams (E3)

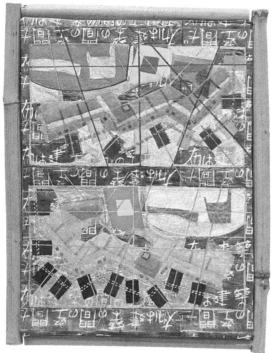
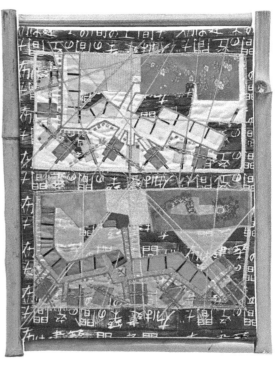

Fabric, the Space between Architecture I, II, III, IV—a Quadtych
by Randell L. Duggins Jr.
2007, each panel 12″ × 16″

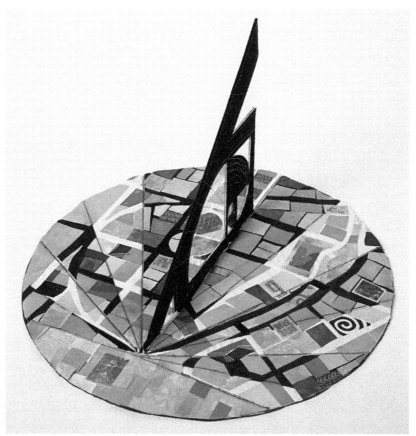

A Nolli Sundial
by Theri Andino
2007, 17″ in diameter

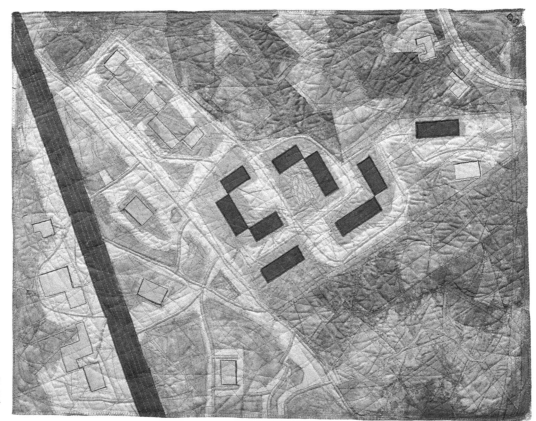

Ella Luna by
Susan Lee Marston
2011, 24″ × 18″

Sweet Summer Memories
by Elizabeth Dorn Zwiener
2012, 25″ × 18″

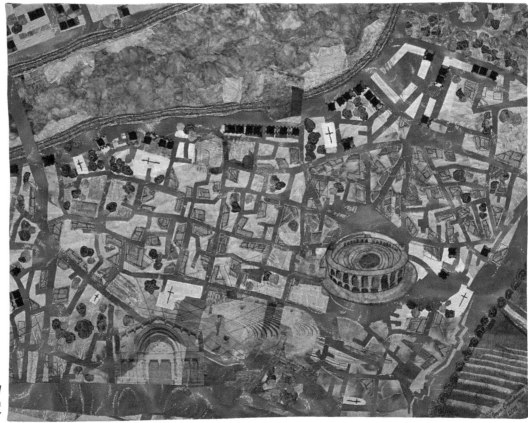

Arles, Interpreted
by Joyce Copenhagen
2012, 37½″ × 30″

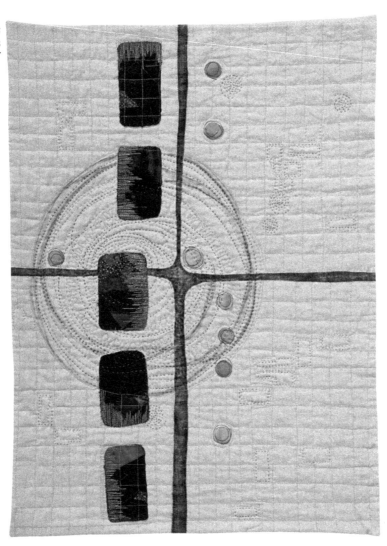

Crossroads
by Catherine Nicholls
2012, 23″ × 31″

South Haven, Michigan
by Julie Rivera
2012, 19″ × 13″

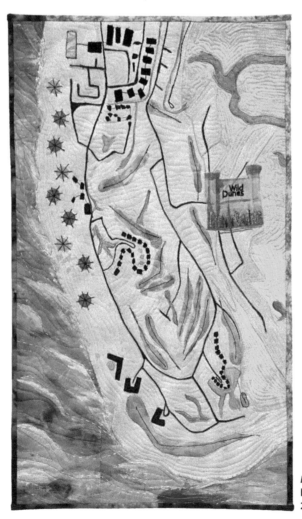

A Place Called Home
by Jerome L. Miller II
2011, 24″ × 18″

Family Vacations
by Linda Stegall
2012, 13″ × 19″

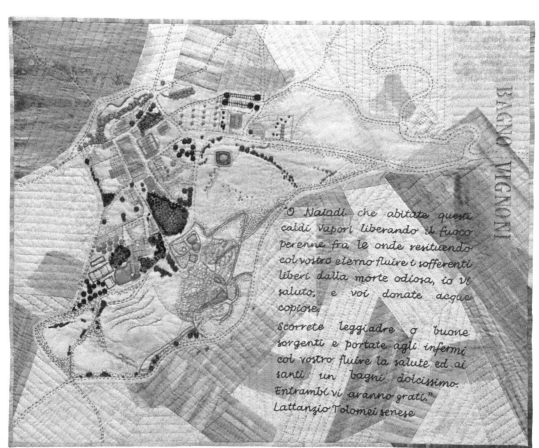

Granville Island
by Bonnie Adie
2012, 35″ × 23″

Bagno Vignoni—
San Quirico d'Orica
by Wendy Osenton
2012, 34″ × 27″

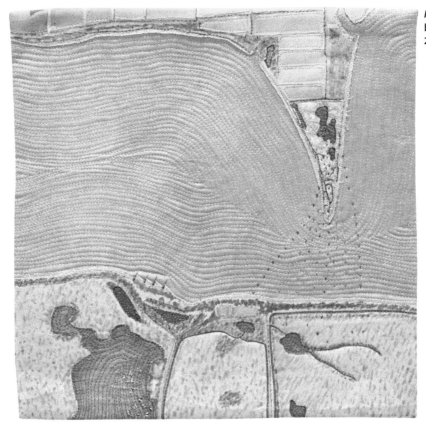

Pathways Home
by Nancy G. Cook
2012, 12″ × 12″

The Spirit of Junkanoo:
From Colour to Life
by Dario McPhee
2011, 23½″ × 18″

Out of the Box
by Sandra E. Lauterbach
2012, 43″ × 37″

Red Touch
by Dezmond Ardis
2011, 23″ × 17¼″

resources

Liquitex Designer Six Acrylic Paint

Liquitex Fabric Medium

Fabrico Dual-Tip Fabric Markers

Derwent Inktense Pencils

These paints and art supplies available at your local art supply or craft store, or online

Mistyfuse Fusible Web

Available at quilt shops or from www.mistyfuse.com

Silk Organza

Dharma Trading Co.
www.dharmatrading.com

Silicone Release Paper

C&T Publishing, Inc.
www.ctpub.com

MY FAVORITE BOOKS ABOUT DESIGN, MAPS, AND ARCHITECTURE

101 Things I Learned in Architecture School by Matthew Frederick

Design Language by Tim McCreight

Designs on the Land: Exploring America from the Air by Alex MacLean

The Map as Art: Contemporary Artists Explore Cartography by Katharine Harmon

Paula Scher: MAPS by Paula Scher

Personal Geographies: Explorations in Mixed-Media Mapmaking by Jill K. Berry

Principles of Form and Design by Wucius Wong

You Are Here: Personal Geographies and Other Maps of the Imagination by Katharine Harmon

about the author

Valerie S. Goodwin received degrees in architecture from Washington University in St. Louis and Yale University. She lives in Tallahassee, Florida, and teaches architectural design at Florida A&M University. Valerie has a studio space in a popular warehouse area for artists near the campus where she teaches.

She became very interested in designing and making quilts in 1998 as an outgrowth of her architectural background. The pursuit began as part of an investigation in the design classes that she teaches, in which she asked students to explore parallels between architecture and quilting. They studied issues related to composition, ordering systems, color, and pattern. What began as a teaching tool became a passion and grew into a successful career as a fiber artist.

Her award-winning work has been widely published and exhibited. She gives lectures and workshops nationally and internationally. Most of her work is inspired by her love of aerial views of landscapes and cities. Many of her quilts are based on maps. Her art has moved through various stages from traditional quilting to an interest in abstract expressionism. However, she is most passionate about creating work inspired by real and imaginary landscapes and cities.

Find out more about her workshops, lectures, and commissions at her website, www.quiltsbyvalerie.com.

Great Titles and Products

from C&T PUBLISHING

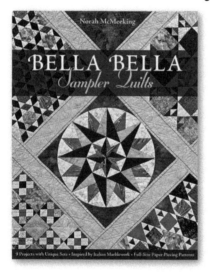

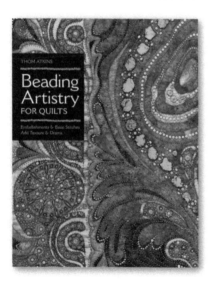

Available at your local retailer or **www.ctpub.com** *or* **800-284-1114**

For a list of other fine books from C&T Publishing, visit our website
to view our catalog online.

C&T PUBLISHING, INC.

P.O. Box 1456
Lafayette, CA 94549
800-284-1114

Email: ctinfo@ctpub.com
Website: www.ctpub.com

C&T Publishing's professional photography services are now available to
the public. Visit us at www.ctmediaservices.com.

Tips and Techniques can be found at www.ctpub.com > Consumer
Resources > Quiltmaking Basics: Tips & Techniques for Quiltmaking & More

For quilting supplies:

COTTON PATCH

1025 Brown Ave.
Lafayette, CA 94549
Store: 925-284-1177
Mail order: 925-283-7883

Email: CottonPa@aol.com
Website: www.quiltusa.com

Note: Fabrics shown may not be currently available, as fabric
manufacturers keep most fabrics in print for only a short time.

Printed in the USA
CPSIA information can be obtained
at www.ICGtesting.com
LVHW062154170624
783427LV00048B/2182

9 781607 056829